BEST OF THE BEST *Presents*

GREAT FOOD FAST

BOB WARDEN'S ULTIMATE PRESSURE COOKER RECIPES

BOB WARDEN

with CHRISTIAN STELLA

QUAIL RIDGE PRESS
Preserving America's Food Heritage

Published by Quail Ridge Press and Great Chefs International

First printing, December 2011 • Second, December 2011
Third, February 2012 • Fourth, December 2012 • Fifth, January 2013
Sixth, April 2013

Authors:
Bob Warden
with Christian Stella

Author photograph ©Benoit Cortet

Book Design and Food Photography by
Christian and Elise Stella

ISBN 978-1-934193-79-2

Manufactured in the USA

CONTENTS

Foreword

by Gwen McKee

When Bob Warden asked me years ago to do a pressure cooker cookbook with him (following our successful collaboration on the *Best of the Best Cook's Essentials Cookbook*), I respectfully declined due to inexperience. "I haven't owned a pressure cooker in years," I said. So he sent me one, and he promised I'd love it. But as a Louisiana gal who grew up on stove-top sautéing and simmering, I was more than a little skeptical.

For those of you who don't already know, Bob Warden is an accomplished chef with cooking experience that spans the globe. He knows, imagines, creates, and/or procures the essentials needed for good cooking. He became my good friend because we both like to cook and eat and because we both love to share what we've learned about cooking with others.

The first pressure cooker that I ever used was a wedding present, and it was an old-fashioned stove-top cooker that had one of those little buoy-looking bobbles on the lid. It never failed to cause me fear and trepidation when using it. In fact, it came with warnings from my mother, who wouldn't let my sisters and me get anywhere near her own pressure cooker as we grew up. These memories stuck with me, and I rarely broke out my wedding present because of it. Of course, before microwaving made thawing a whole lot faster, the pressure cooker was my emergency cookware of choice when dinner was forgotten in the freezer.

But when Bob sent me a new and modern cook's essentials® pressure cooker, I was like a kid with a brand-new toy! It was so easy to use that, almost immediately, I was turning out great dishes in far less time than even I thought possible. Who would have thought it could make such a difference in my kitchen? With no more fear of that little buoy thing being knocked off and spewing volcanically onto the ceiling, I go boldly forward, understanding why so many people cook with pressure cookers these days. Not only do I enjoy using mine...I am hooked!

But let's talk about cookbooks, which just so happen to be my favorite books in the world. Having produced hundreds, I am forever testing recipes, and I know how a great recipe can make you feel like you've stumbled onto something magical. When it comes to pressure cooking, recipes can help us demystify and deconstruct the process, no matter what our skill set may be. Pressure cooking, like baking, is a science. It's important to use the right ingredients in the right amounts and cook them for the right amount of time, under the right amount of pressure. For these reasons alone, I endorse this cookbook. Bob is very dedicated and thorough in whatever he does, and this cookbook is no exception. The recipes are creative and taste great. The recipes have been tested, edited—and most importantly—they work!

If pressure cooking is a science, Bob is one of those teachers who is so down to earth that he can make you forget all about that...he can make you feel empowered in the kitchen. This cookbook—especially Bob's directions and tips—should help take the pressure off your pressure cooking. I know it did for me.

Always my best,
Gwen McKee

Introduction

Demystifying Pressure Cooking

As Gwen just touched on in the preceding Foreword, pressure cooking has come a very long way in recent years. No longer do we need to worry about the confusing and sometimes frightening stove-top pressure cookers and their tendency to burn food when not watched carefully enough. Today, digital pressure cookers can literally take all of the pressure off of this great (and extremely fast!) way of cooking.

I like to think that my last pressure cooking cookbook, *Slow Food Fast*, helped demystify pressure cooking even further. I had been presenting the ease of pressure cookers on TV for years, but I soon realized that I needed to compile a cookbook that gave the clearest and most concise directions for delicious food that I could muster. Simply put, too many pressure cooker cookbooks read like technical manuals or textbooks, and nearly all of them contain no photographs whatsoever. Call me old fashioned, but I like to eat with my eyes first! While I had always set out to create the first true companion to the digital pressure cookers I demonstrate on TV, I was still deeply humbled by the success and kind reviews I received for that book.

When it came time to sit down and write an all-new pressure cooking book, I decided to take my goal of demystifying pressure cooking even further. I decided to stop and read each and every Internet review, forum, and blog post ever written about my last book and give my fans exactly what they wanted. I even decided to push the limits of pressure cooking and try things I've never seen or thought could be prepared that way (like lasagna!). The result is the book you have in your hands. It has been a labor of love more than two years in the making. It contains recipes that I consider to be the best I've ever written.

There's an element of surprise to pressure cooking. You put everything in the pot, close it up, and let it cook sight unseen. It isn't until you've released the pressure and opened that lid, until you've dipped a spoon in and had a taste, that you truly know what you have. I can tell you that I am still surprised when I open that lid. I've tested some of the recipes in this book a dozen times and that moment—that first spoonful—still gets me.

How to Adjust Recipes for PSI

While the recipes in this book were written and tested in cook's essentials® Digital Pressure Cookers, they can be prepared in any pressure cooker, whether digital or stove top.

Some cookers display the cooking pressure in the simple terms of "HIGH" and "LOW," while other cookers display them in "psi" (pounds per square inch). Most of the recipes in this book are written to be cooked under the highest pressure—HIGH on some models of pressure cookers and 15psi on others. The few recipes in this book that are labeled to cook on LOW pressure should be cooked at 7.5psi on cookers that display in psi.

Before using any pressure cooker for the first time, it is highly recommended that you read that cooker's manual from front to back to fully understand how to safely and correctly operate it.

Quick and Natural Releases

When using a pressure cooker, there are two methods to release the pressure after cooking. This book uses both of these methods, depending on the needs of the recipe. A "quick release" typically involves opening a steam valve to let the pressure escape all at once. A "natural release" is when you simply let the cooker sit until the pressure naturally dissipates on its own. This natural release process can take up to 15 minutes. For many cookers, it is not immediately obvious when a cooker has naturally released all pressure, so I usually include how long to let the cooker sit and naturally release pressure before quick releasing the remaining pressure to get the optimum results. For more information on how to perform quick releases with your specific cooker, be sure to consult your manual. I highly recommend using an oven mitt to quick release to keep your hand safe from any hot steam. Loosely placing a towel over the steam valve can soak up the steam and keep it from collecting on your walls or cabinets.

About Cooking Times

Cooking times at the top of the recipe pages in this book refer to the amount of time the recipes cook under pressure and do not include the time it takes your particular cooker to come up to pressure or the time it may take to brown meats or sauté vegetables. It was decided that simplifying the cooking time to the time under pressure will allow you to easily glance at the page and accurately set the timer on a digital pressure cooker. Please assume that all recipes will take an additional 5–15 minutes to come up to pressure. While this may seem long, keep in mind that it is no different from the time it takes to preheat an oven.

Cooking from Frozen

One of the biggest things I overlooked in my last pressure cooking book was that using a pressure cooker allows you to cook certain cuts of meat directly out of the freezer. While I decided to write the recipes with fresh or thawed cuts of meat in mind (unless otherwise noted), I now include a column in the pressure cooking time charts at the back of the book that shows the adjustment time for cooking cuts of meat like chicken breasts and pork chops from frozen. This adjustment time can be added to any recipe using that cut of meat in the book, though you will need to skip any browning of the meat. As you cannot brown frozen meat, cooking from fresh will usually yield the best flavor, but the option to cook from frozen is now easily looked up when you're in a pinch.

Cooking frozen cuts of meat is not recommended when following a recipe that contains potatoes, delicate vegetables, pasta, or rice, as it will result in overcooking the other components of the dish.

Using Bases

One of the principals of good cooking, especially pressure cooking, is that you should never miss an opportunity to add flavor. It is for this reason that you may notice that nearly all of the recipes in this book use stocks or broths in place of water. Creating your own stock (while delicious) can be quite time consuming, and purchasing cans or cartons of pre-made stock or broth can get very expensive. This is where bases come in.

I highly suggest purchasing beef, chicken, and vegetable bases to prepare the recipes in this book. A highly concentrated liquid or paste, these bases can be diluted (according to the jar or bottle's directions) to create instant stocks. While these bases may seem expensive at first, compare the cups of stock they will create with the costs of purchasing regular stock or broth, and you will find that you are saving quite a lot of money in the end.

Additionally, these bases tend to be far, far lower in sodium than other, less natural options like bouillon cubes. The other advantage of bases is that you can add more base to taste for more robust sauces that taste like they've been reducing on the stove all day long. While none of the recipes in this book require you to add any extra base than the package's recommended ratio, many of the gravies in these recipes will taste even better if you add an extra teaspoon or so to taste before serving.

I wholeheartedly recommend **Great Flavors** brand bases.

Nutrition

While providing nutritional analysis of my recipes has been a request I've heard often, the decision was made to only include that information in the "Lighter Fare" category of this book. There were several deciding factors that influenced this decision, the biggest of which was that several of the recipes in this book give you the option of choosing from multiple cuts of meat that have completely different nutritional breakdowns.

Beyond that, many of these recipes create cooking liquid that is drained, or a larger amount of gravy than is likely to be eaten. In recipes such as The Whole Bird, a whole cooked chicken is removed from the cooking liquid containing olive oil and the cooked-down chicken fat. While you may drizzle a spoonful of this cooking liquid over the carved chicken to keep it moist, it is very unlikely that you would consume all two cups of the liquid. Current recipe analysis software is unable to account for this and will simply add everything together, disregarding that most of the fat in that recipe is being left in the pot.

The nutritional information provided in the "Lighter Fare" category of this book was calculated using software that accesses the USDA database. The information on each page is for one serving of the recipe, and it was calculated by tabulating all combined ingredients and dividing by the number of servings in the recipe. This means that, as explained above, these numbers do include all cooking liquid and/or gravy created in the cooking process. Inconsistencies in cuts of meat and different brands of ingredients vary in nutritional breakdown, so these numbers are only included as a rough guide.

While some of the other recipes in this book offer suggestions on cutting down fat and calories, the best way to cut down on fat is to simply look for cuts of meat that have less fat marbled throughout, and trim any excess fat before cooking. This may affect the tenderness of the meat, but that's nothing that cooking a few additional minutes under pressure can't fix!

For those interested in reducing sodium in these recipes, it is highly suggested that you use the low-sodium versions of stocks/broths, soy sauce, and other condiments. Any actual salt used in any recipe in this book can be reduced, omitted, or replaced with a salt substitute, depending on your taste or dietary needs.

Pantry Shopping List

This is a list of the most commonly used ingredients in the recipes in this book. In testing the recipes, we found that by stocking up on many of these essentials, you should be able to prepare nearly any recipe in this book for under $15.00.

Spice Rack

Allspice, Ground

Bay Leaves

Chili Powder

Cinnamon, Ground

Cumin, Ground

Dried Oregano

Dried Thyme

Garlic Powder

Italian Seasoning

Mustard, Ground

Nutmeg

Onion Powder

Paprika

Poultry Seasoning

Salt and Pepper

White Pepper

Cupboard

All-Purpose Flour

Apple Cider Vinegar

Arborio Rice

Balsamic Vinegar

Barbecue Sauce

Beef base or broth

Chicken base or broth

Chunky Salsa

Chunky Spaghetti Sauce, Jarred

Coarse-Ground Mustard

Cornstarch

Diced Tomatoes, Canned

Dijon Mustard

Evaporated Milk

Honey

Ketchup

Lemon Juice

Light Brown Sugar

Minced Garlic, Jarred

Olive Oil

Sugar

Tomato Paste

Vanilla Extract

Vegetable Base or Broth

Vegetable Oil

White Wine

Worcestershire Sauce

Fridge

Bell Peppers

Butter or Margarine

Carrots

Celery

Eggs

Fresh Herbs

Half-and-Half

Heavy Cream

Lemons

Milk

Parmesan Cheese, Grated

Red Onions

Tomatoes

Yellow Onions (Sweet)

SOUPS
AND
STARTERS

Tortellini and Meatball Soup

SOUPS

Like Italian Wedding, with Cheese-Filled Tortellini

This variation on the classic wedding soup has full-sized meatballs and cheese-filled tortellini in place of the miniature ingredients in most recipes.

SHOPPING LIST

2 tablespoons olive oil

1 yellow onion, thinly sliced

1 cup sliced celery

6 cups chicken stock or broth

1 (16-ounce) bag frozen Italian meatballs

1 (8-ounce) bag dried cheese tortellini

2 cups chopped kale

1 tablespoon minced garlic

Juice of ½ lemon

1 teaspoon sugar

1 teaspoon dried basil

Salt and pepper

1 WITH the cooker's lid off, heat oil on HIGH or "brown," until sizzling.

2 PLACE onion in the cooker, and sauté until translucent, about 5 minutes.

3 ADD celery, chicken stock, meatballs, tortellini, kale, garlic, lemon juice, sugar, and basil.

4 SECURELY lock the pressure cooker's lid and set for 5 minutes on HIGH.

5 PERFORM a quick release to release the cooker's pressure.

6 ADD salt and pepper to taste before serving.

HELPFUL TIP

Fresh spinach leaves can be used in place of the kale, if desired.

SOUPS

Five Alarm Chili

Serve with Ice Water... Plenty of Ice Water

I must warn you that this spicy chili recipe is not for the faint of heart! Topping your bowl with a large dollop of sour cream will help you cool things down though.

SHOPPING LIST

1 ¼ cups kidney beans (not canned)

3 tablespoons vegetable oil

2 pounds lean ground beef

1 large red onion, chopped

3 tablespoons chili powder

2 jalapeño peppers, diced (with seeds)

2 (15-ounce) cans diced tomatoes

1 (28-ounce) can tomato sauce

2 cups beef stock or broth

1 tablespoon minced garlic

2 teaspoons sugar

1 teaspoon ground cayenne pepper

1 teaspoon ground cumin

1 ½ teaspoons salt

½ teaspoon pepper

1 (16-ounce) bag frozen corn kernels

1 SOAK kidney beans for 30 minutes as you prep the remaining ingredients. Drain and rinse the soaked beans.

2 WITH the cooker's lid off, heat oil on HIGH or "brown," until melted and sizzling.

3 PLACE the ground beef and onion in the cooker, and cook until ground beef is lightly browned, about 7 minutes.

4 STIR in chili powder and jalapeño peppers, and cook 1 additional minute.

5 ADD remaining ingredients, except frozen corn. Securely lock the pressure cooker's lid and set for 26 minutes on HIGH.

6 LET the pressure release naturally for 10 minutes before performing a quick release for any remaining pressure.

7 SET cooker to HIGH or "brown," and stir in frozen corn kernels. Let simmer 3 minutes before serving.

MAKE IT FASTER

Substitute 1 (15-ounce) can of kidney beans (drained) in place of the dried beans and you can reduce the cooking time to only 8 minutes on HIGH!

Broccoli and Cheese Soup

My Take on a Universal Favorite

Just about everyone loves this creamy vegetable soup, because broccoli and cheese are simply star-crossed, destined to belong together. Sweet yellow onion and strips of vibrant carrots give this amazing appetizer even more texture and flavor.

SHOPPING LIST

2 tablespoons butter or margarine

1 yellow onion, diced

Florets of 1 large bunch broccoli, chopped

1 cup shredded carrots

4 cups chicken stock or broth

¼ teaspoon garlic powder

¼ teaspoon onion powder

1 cup heavy cream

1 ¼ cups shredded sharp Cheddar cheese

Salt and pepper

1 WITH the cooker's lid off, heat butter on HIGH or "brown," until melted and sizzling.

2 PLACE onion in cooker and sauté until translucent, 4–5 minutes.

3 ADD broccoli florets, carrots, chicken stock, garlic powder, and onion powder. Securely lock the pressure cooker's lid and set for 4 minutes on HIGH.

4 PERFORM a quick release to release the cooker's pressure.

5 STIR in heavy cream and Cheddar cheese, and then add salt and pepper to taste before serving.

MAKE IT MY WAY

Though not everyone is a fan of nutmeg, I like to add just a tiny pinch to Broccoli and Cheese Soup for a hint of nuttiness.

Corn Off the Cob Soup

SOUPS

Just Don't Try to Eat It with Your Hands

This soup, one of my absolute favorites, is bursting with fresh, buttery corn flavor. I like to prepare it with half yellow corn and half white corn for an even nicer presentation.

SHOPPING LIST

1 tablespoon vegetable oil

1 small yellow onion, diced

5 cups fresh corn kernels, cut off the cob

3 cups chicken stock or broth

2 teaspoons sugar

¾ teaspoon salt

¼ teaspoon garlic powder

½ teaspoon dried thyme

2 tablespoons cornstarch

1 (12-ounce) can evaporated milk

3 tablespoons butter or margarine

¼ cup finely diced red bell pepper

1 WITH the cooker's lid off, heat oil on HIGH or "brown," until sizzling.

2 PLACE the onion in the cooker, and cook until lightly caramelized, about 5 minutes.

3 ADD corn, chicken stock, sugar, salt, garlic powder, and thyme, securely lock the pressure cooker's lid, and set for 6 minutes on HIGH.

4 PERFORM a quick release to release the cooker's pressure. Set the cooker to HIGH or "brown."

5 WHISK the cornstarch into the evaporated milk and stir into the soup. Let simmer 2 minutes, or until thickened.

6 STIR in butter and diced red bell pepper, and cook 1 additional minute before serving.

MAKE IT BETTER

For a thicker, creamier soup, use a hand blender (or transfer half of the soup to a food processor or blender) to partially purée the corn kernels before adding the cornstarch and evaporated milk.

Sausage and Spinach Soup

with Sliced Potatoes

Robust flavors truly define this very simple soup, packed with fresh spinach leaves, Italian sausage, and hunks of potato.

SHOPPING LIST

2 tablespoons olive oil

1 pound ground Italian sausage

1 red onion, diced

6 cups chicken stock or broth

1 (10-ounce) bag fresh
spinach leaves

5 redskin potatoes, thickly sliced

1 tablespoon minced garlic

1 teaspoon sugar

1 teaspoon Italian seasoning

¼ teaspoon crushed red pepper

1 bay leaf

½ cup heavy cream

Salt and pepper

1 WITH the cooker's lid off, heat oil on HIGH or "brown," until sizzling.

2 PLACE sausage and onion in the cooker, and sauté until sausage is browned and onion is translucent.

3 ADD chicken stock, spinach leaves, potatoes, garlic, sugar, Italian seasoning, crushed red pepper, and bay leaf.

4 SECURELY lock the pressure cooker's lid and set for 3 minutes on HIGH.

5 PERFORM a quick release to release the cooker's pressure.

6 STIR in heavy cream, and add salt and pepper to taste before serving.

HELPFUL TIP

If your store does not carry ground Italian sausage in bulk, simply buy Italian sausage links and slice the casings off before preparing.

Prep Time	Cook Time	Temperature	Serves
20 min	12 min	High	6

Chicken and Wild Rice Soup

With a Rich and Creamy Broth

This classic soup can be made in a pressure cooker from prep to finish in less time than it would take to simply cook plain wild rice on the stove. When shopping, look for real, uncooked wild rice with long black grains—not a wild rice pilaf or mix.

SHOPPING LIST

1 pound boneless, skinless chicken thighs, cubed

3 tablespoons all-purpose flour

Salt and pepper

3 tablespoons butter or margarine

1 tablespoon vegetable oil

1 yellow onion, diced

4 stalks celery, chopped

2 large carrots, chopped

8 fresh sage leaves, chopped

1 teaspoon dried thyme

1 ¼ cups wild rice

6 cups chicken stock or broth

1 cup heavy cream

1 tomato, diced

CUT THE COST

Any cut of boneless chicken will work in this recipe, so feel free to buy 1 pound of chicken breasts or tenders if they are on sale or less expensive than the thighs.

1 Toss the cubed chicken thighs in flour that has been generously seasoned with salt and pepper, until all pieces are lightly coated.

2 With the cooker's lid off, heat butter and oil on HIGH or "brown," until melted and sizzling.

3 Place the coated chicken in the cooker, and cook until lightly browned, about 5 minutes.

4 Add the onion, celery, carrots, sage, and thyme and stir well, cooking 1 additional minute.

5 Cover all with wild rice and chicken stock, securely lock the pressure cooker's lid, and set for 12 minutes on HIGH.

6 Let the pressure release naturally for 10 minutes before performing a quick release for any remaining pressure.

7 Stir in heavy cream, diced tomato, and salt and pepper to taste before serving.

Prep Time	Cook Time	Temperature	Serves
20 min	8 min	High	6

French Onion Soup

A Restaurant Favorite Recreated in Record Time

French Onion Soup is one of those restaurant staples that seems so simple to prepare, yet there's one ingredient that keeps most of us from even bothering to prepare it at home...time. Restaurants love to serve this soup because it only gets better and better as it sits on the warmer. Using a pressure cooker, you can infuse that same flavor without all of those hours on a hot plate!

SHOPPING LIST

3 tablespoons butter

1 tablespoon vegetable oil

3 large yellow onions, thinly sliced

2 teaspoons light brown sugar

4 cups beef stock or broth

1 cup dry red wine, may substitute beef stock

1 teaspoon dried thyme

1 bay leaf

¼ teaspoon garlic powder

1 teaspoon salt

½ teaspoon pepper

2 cups crunchy croutons

6 slices provolone cheese

PLAY IT SAFE

These soup crocks will be HOT out of the broiler! Be sure to use oven mitts to transfer each to a plate lined with a napkin before serving. Most of all—be sure to warn your guests!

1 WITH the cooker's lid off, heat butter and oil on HIGH or "brown," until sizzling.

2 PLACE onions and sugar in the cooker, and cook until the onions caramelize, 10–12 minutes.

3 ADD the beef stock, wine, thyme, bay leaf, garlic powder, salt, and pepper and stir to combine.

4 SECURELY lock the pressure cooker's lid and set for 8 minutes on HIGH.

5 PERFORM a quick release to release the cooker's pressure.

6 SET your oven's broiler to HIGH and place 6 oven-safe soup crocks on a large sheet pan. Ladle the onion soup (with plenty of onions) into each crock, filling until about ½ inch from the top.

7 COMPLETELY cover the surface of each crock of soup with croutons and then place a slice of provolone cheese over top. Carefully place sheet pan of soup crocks under broiler and cook until cheese is bubbling and beginning to brown, 3–5 minutes.

Prep Time	Cook Time	Temperature	Serves
30 min	24 min	High	6

Steak Chili

A Hearty Chili That's Fit for a Meal

This steak chili made with fresh pinto beans makes a warm and satisfying meal, especially when served over rice or pasta. I like to use sirloin steak but cheaper cuts of beef, especially cubed stewing beef, work great too.

SHOPPING LIST

1 ¼ cups pinto beans (not canned)

3 tablespoons vegetable oil

1 ½ pounds sirloin steaks, cubed

1 large yellow onion, chopped

1 tablespoon chili powder

1 green bell pepper chopped

3 large tomatoes, chopped

1 (28-ounce) can tomato sauce

5 cups beef stock or broth

1 tablespoon minced garlic

2 teaspoons sugar

½ teaspoon salt

¼ teaspoon pepper

MAKE IT YOURS

Serve this chili smothered with your favorite toppings. Try Cheddar or pepper-jack cheese, sour cream, sliced jalapeños, diced red onion, or even a dollop of guacamole!

1 SOAK pinto beans for 30 minutes as you prep the remaining ingredients. Drain and rinse the soaked beans.

2 WITH the cooker's lid off, heat oil on HIGH or "brown," until melted and sizzling.

3 PLACE the steak and onion in the cooker, and cook until steak is lightly browned, about 5 minutes.

4 STIR in chili powder and cook 1 additional minute.

5 ADD remaining ingredients, securely lock the pressure cooker's lid, and set for 24 minutes on HIGH.

6 LET the pressure release naturally for 10 minutes before performing a quick release for any remaining pressure.

7 ADD any additional salt and pepper to taste before serving.

Prep Time	Cook Time	Temperature	Serves
15 min	5 min	High	6

SOUPS

Hot and Sour Soup

A Far East Favorite

Hot and Sour Soup is always one of the first things I think about when Chinese take-out is mentioned. My version packs quite a kick, though it isn't quite as spicy as some I've come across.

SHOPPING LIST

1 tablespoon sesame oil

1 yellow onion, thinly sliced

8 ounces button mushrooms, quartered

5 cups chicken stock or broth

1 (8-ounce) can sliced water chestnuts

1 (8-ounce) can sliced bamboo shoots

3 tablespoons rice wine vinegar

3 tablespoons low-sodium soy sauce

¼ teaspoon crushed red pepper flakes

¼ teaspoon white pepper

2 tablespoons cornstarch, mixed into 2 tablespoons water

1 (8-ounce) package firm tofu, cubed

3 green onions, thinly sliced

1 WITH the cooker's lid off, heat oil and onion on HIGH or "brown," and sauté until onion is translucent, about 3 minutes.

2 ADD mushrooms, chicken stock, water chestnuts, bamboo shoots, vinegar, soy sauce, crushed red pepper flakes, and white pepper to the cooker.

3 SECURELY lock the pressure cooker's lid and set for 5 minutes on HIGH.

4 PERFORM a quick release to release the cooker's pressure.

5 WITH the cooker's lid off, set to HIGH or "brown." Add the cornstarch mixture and tofu cubes, and simmer 2 minutes.

6 SERVE topped with green onion slices.

HELPFUL TIP

The canned water chestnuts, bamboo shoots, and rice wine vinegar used in this recipe should all be available in the Asian foods section of your local grocery store.

Prep Time	Cook Time	Temperature	Serves
20 min	6 min	High	6

SOUPS

Chicken Noodle Soup

with Bowtie Pasta

This version of a heartwarming staple, known for getting you through a tough cold, keeps things simple, familiar, and as always, delicious. Can opener not necessary.

SHOPPING LIST

1 pound boneless, skinless chicken breasts, cubed

2 tablespoons all-purpose flour

Salt and pepper

3 tablespoons butter or margarine

1 yellow onion, diced

4 ribs celery, sliced

3 large carrots, sliced

1 teaspoon dried thyme

1 ½ cups uncooked farfalle pasta

6 cups chicken stock or broth

½ teaspoon salt

¼ teaspoon pepper

1 cup frozen corn kernels, thawed

1 TOSS the cubed chicken breasts in flour that has been generously seasoned with salt and pepper, until all pieces are lightly coated.

2 WITH the cooker's lid off, heat butter on HIGH or "brown," until melted and sizzling.

3 PLACE the coated chicken in the cooker, and cook until lightly browned, about 5 minutes.

4 ADD the onion, celery, carrots, and thyme, and stir well, cooking 1 additional minute.

5 COVER all with pasta, chicken stock, salt, and pepper. Securely lock the pressure cooker's lid and set for 6 minutes on HIGH.

6 PERFORM a quick release to release the cooker's pressure.

7 STIR in corn kernels and simmer 1 minute before serving.

MAKE IT BETTER

Three sprigs fresh thyme can be used in place of the dried thyme for an even better flavor. Feel free to leave them whole, and simply remove before serving.

Creamy Tomato Basil Soup

To Warm You Through and Through

This simple and satisfying tomato soup takes only 8 minutes of cooking under pressure to taste like it's been simmering on the stove all day long. For the perfect accompaniment, make some quick garlic bread by brushing a halved loaf of Italian bread with olive oil and garlic paste and then broiling 2-3 minutes.

SHOPPING LIST

2 tablespoons butter or margarine

1 tablespoon olive oil

1 yellow onion, diced

1 (28-ounce) can tomato sauce

8 Roma tomatoes, finely diced

4 cups chicken stock or broth

12 large leaves fresh basil, chopped

1 tablespoon minced garlic

1 teaspoon sugar

½ teaspoon Italian seasoning

1 cup heavy cream

Salt and pepper

Grated Parmesan cheese, optional

1 WITH the cooker's lid off, heat butter and oil on HIGH or "brown," until melted and sizzling.

2 PLACE the onion in the cooker, and cook just until translucent, about 5 minutes.

3 COVER with remaining ingredients, except heavy cream, salt and pepper, and Parmesan cheese.

4 SECURELY lock the pressure cooker's lid and set for 8 minutes on HIGH.

5 LET the pressure release naturally for 5 minutes before performing a quick release for any remaining pressure.

6 STIR in heavy cream and a generous amount of salt and pepper to taste. Serve each bowl topped with grated Parmesan cheese, if desired.

MAKE IT MEMORABLE

Place several large leaves of fresh basil atop each other and then roll them all up like a crepe. Thinly slice the rolled basil to create long strips (a chiffonade) to sprinkle over the top of the soup just before serving.

Prep Time	Cook Time	Temperature	Serves
20 min	7 min	High	6

SOUPS

Chicken Tortilla Soup

with Strips of Tender Corn Tortillas

This southwestern soup gives your taste buds a kick before the main course, and while my version is quite traditional, it's done in only seven minutes under pressure.

SHOPPING LIST

1 pound boneless, skinless chicken breasts, cubed

2 tablespoons all-purpose flour

Salt and pepper

2 tablespoons olive oil

1 red onion, diced

2 large carrots, sliced

1 red bell pepper, diced

1 small jalapeño pepper, seeded and diced

5 cups chicken stock or broth

3 tablespoons chopped fresh cilantro

¼ teaspoon ground cumin

½ teaspoon salt

¼ teaspoon pepper

1 cup frozen corn kernels, thawed

4 soft corn tortillas, cut into thin strips

1 Toss the cubed chicken breasts in flour that has been generously seasoned with salt and pepper, until all pieces are lightly coated.

2 With the cooker's lid off, heat oil on HIGH or "brown," until sizzling.

3 Place the coated chicken in the cooker and sauté until lightly browned, about 5 minutes.

4 Add the onion, carrots, bell pepper, and jalapeño pepper, and stir well, sautéing 1 additional minute.

5 Add the chicken stock, cilantro, cumin, salt, and pepper to the chicken mixture. Securely lock the pressure cooker's lid and set for 7 minutes on HIGH.

6 Perform a quick release to release the cooker's pressure. Stir in corn kernels and tortilla strips before serving.

MAKE IT YOURS

If you like things spicy, keep the seeds intact when preparing the jalapeño, and add 1 tablespoon hot pepper sauce in step 5.

Prep Time	Cook Time	Temperature	Serves
30 min	8 min	High	6

SOUPS

Porcupine Meatballs

Rice Stuffed Meatballs in a Sweet Tomato Sauce

These slightly sweet meatballs could easily become a household favorite, with a very low cook time and a kid-friendly flavor. No need to cook the rice beforehand!

SHOPPING LIST

½ cup long-grain white rice (uncooked)

¼ cup finely diced yellow onion

¼ cup beef stock or broth

1 teaspoon Worcestershire sauce

¼ teaspoon garlic powder

⅛ teaspoon allspice

1 ¼ teaspoons salt

¼ teaspoon pepper

1 pound ground beef or turkey

2 tablespoons vegetable oil

1 (16-ounce) jar chunky spaghetti sauce

⅔ cup beef stock or broth

3 teaspoons sugar

HELPFUL TIP

Loosely pile the meatballs in the cooker, otherwise they may weigh each other down and lose their shape.

1 IN a mixing bowl, combine uncooked rice, onion, beef broth, Worcestershire sauce, garlic powder, allspice, salt, and pepper. Add the ground beef (or turkey) to the bowl and fold in, mixing well.

2 FORM the meat mixture into 1 ½ inch balls.

3 WITH the cooker's lid off, heat oil on HIGH or "brown," until sizzling.

4 PLACE meatballs in the oil in pressure cooker and brown on at least 2 sides. You will most likely need to work in multiple batches to brown them all. Once finished, return all batches to the cooker.

5 POUR spaghetti sauce, beef broth, and sugar over meatballs in cooker and securely lock the pressure cooker's lid. Set for 8 minutes on HIGH.

6 LET the pressure release naturally 10 minutes before performing a quick release for any remaining pressure. Set cooker to LOW or "warm" and serve right out of the pot.

SOUPS

Taco Dip

All the Good Stuff, Just Served the Fun Way

This party dip has everything you'd stuff inside a taco shell: refried beans, salsa, cheese, and sour cream. I've added just a couple of jalapeño peppers to give it a kick.

SHOPPING LIST

1 tablespoon vegetable oil

1 pound lean ground beef

1 red onion, diced

1 (16-ounce) jar chunky salsa

2 jalapeño peppers, seeded and finely diced

2 teaspoons chili powder

½ teaspoon ground cumin

2 tablespoons chopped fresh cilantro

1 (16-ounce) can refried beans

1 cup sour cream

1 cup shredded sharp Cheddar cheese

Salt and pepper

1 WITH the cooker's lid off, heat oil on HIGH or "brown," until sizzling.

2 PLACE beef and onion in the cooker, and sauté until beef has browned, 5–7 minutes. Drain well.

3 ADD salsa, jalapeño peppers, chili powder, cumin, and cilantro to the beef in the cooker. Securely lock the pressure cooker's lid and set for 5 minutes on HIGH.

4 PERFORM a quick release to release the cooker's pressure.

5 STIR in refried beans, sour cream, and Cheddar cheese. Add salt and pepper to taste before serving alongside nacho chips.

HELPFUL TIP

When using an electric pressure cooker, you can set the cooker to warm and serve this dip right out of the pot with no worries of it cooling down.

Toasted Walnut Hummus

for Your Dipping Pleasure

Cooked, mashed chickpeas offer quite a smooth experience for any pita chip, and tossing in a whole lot of toasted walnut goodness adds something a bit extra to this Middle Eastern spread.

SHOPPING LIST

3 cups dried chickpeas

2 tablespoons vegetable oil

1 cup chopped walnuts

⅓ cup olive oil

Juice of 1 lemon

1 tablespoon minced garlic

1 tablespoon chopped parsley

2 teaspoons light brown sugar

1 teaspoon coriander

Salt and pepper

HELPFUL TIP

To control the consistency of the hummus, it is best to add the olive oil a little bit at a time, until the dip is exactly to your liking.

1 PLACE chickpeas and vegetable oil in cooker, and fill with enough water to cover the peas by 2 inches.

2 SECURELY lock the pressure cooker's lid and set for 35 minutes on HIGH.

3 LET the pressure release naturally for 15 minutes before performing a quick release for any remaining pressure.

4 MEANWHILE, toast walnuts by heating in a large skillet over medium heat for 3–4 minutes, shaking the pan, just until walnuts are fragrant.

5 DRAIN chickpeas, and transfer to a food processor. Add toasted walnuts and remaining ingredients, and pulse until the mixture is smooth.

6 BEFORE serving, season with a generous amount of salt and pepper to taste.

Prep Time	Cook Time	Temperature	Serves
15 min	10 min	High	8

SOUPS

Game Day Sausage Dip

A Creamy Dip with Spicy Pork Sausage

Who ever said you had to be limited to salsa? With a spicy kick infused right into the sausage and a good amount of cooling cream cheese, this dip will surely keep any get-together going.

SHOPPING LIST

1 tablespoon vegetable oil

1 pound spicy ground pork sausage

1 yellow onion, diced

1 (10-ounce) can diced tomatoes with green chiles

½ cup beef stock or broth

2 teaspoons minced garlic

16 ounces (2 bricks) cream cheese

HELPFUL TIP

When using an electric pressure cooker, you can set the cooker to warm and serve this dip right out of the pot with no worries of it cooling down.

1 WITH the cooker's lid off, heat oil on HIGH or "brown," until sizzling.

2 PLACE the sausage and onion in the cooker, and sauté until sausage has browned, 5–7 minutes. Drain well.

3 STIR in tomatoes with green chilies, beef broth, and minced garlic, and securely lock the pressure cooker's lid. Set for 10 minutes on HIGH.

4 LET the pressure release naturally 5 minutes before performing a quick release to release any remaining pressure. Drain off ½ cup of the cooking liquid.

5 WITH the cooker's lid off, set to HIGH or "brown," and stir in cream cheese before serving alongside tortilla chips.

SOUPS

Black-Eyed Pea Dip

A Southern Alternative to a Hummus-Style Dip

This delicious dip marries the style of Greek hummus with the flavors of the United States South, with diced pimentos in place of roasted red peppers that often garnishes hummus.

SHOPPING LIST

1 ½ cups black-eyed peas

2 tablespoons vegetable oil

Juice of ½ lemon

2 tablespoons extra-virgin olive oil

2 teaspoons minced garlic

3 tablespoons diced pimentos

1 tablespoon chopped fresh parsley

1 teaspoon sugar

½ teaspoon salt

PLAY IT SAFE

Though it may seem superfluous, adding oil to the cooker with the peas prevents them from foaming, which can clog the cooker's pressure release valve.

1 PLACE black-eyed peas and vegetable oil in cooker, and fill with enough water to cover the peas by 2 inches.

2 SECURELY lock the pressure cooker's lid and set for 14 minutes on HIGH.

3 LET the pressure release naturally 5 minutes before performing a quick release for any remaining pressure.

4 DRAIN peas and return to cooker. Using a heavy fork or potato masher, mash peas until mostly smooth, adding lemon juice and olive oil as you go.

5 STIR in remaining ingredients before serving warm.

BEEF

Perfected Pot Roast

My Best Pot Roast Recipe Ever

Since everyone can appreciate a good pot roast recipe, I've taken it upon myself to make my best even better, ready to serve in only an hour under pressure.

SHOPPING LIST

1 (2- to 3-pound) beef chuck roast

3 tablespoons all-purpose flour

Salt and pepper

2 tablespoons olive oil

1 ½ cups beef stock or broth

2 tablespoons balsamic vinegar

1 tablespoon minced garlic

1 teaspoon dry thyme

2 bay leaves

1 teaspoon salt

¼ teaspoon pepper

6 redskin potatoes, halved

1 yellow onion, cut into wedges

2 cups baby carrots

2 ribs celery, cut into 1-inch lengths

1 tablespoon cornstarch, mixed into

2 tablespoons water

3 tablespoons butter or margarine

MAKE IT BETTER

I like to add ¼ cup of a dry red wine to the cooker in step 3, which gives an even meatier flavor.

1 SPRINKLE the chuck roast with flour that has been generously seasoned with salt and pepper.

2 WITH the cooker's lid off, heat oil on HIGH or "brown," until sizzling. Place the floured roast in the cooker and brown on each side.

3 ADD the beef broth, vinegar, garlic, thyme, bay leaves, salt, and pepper to the cooker. Securely lock the cooker's lid and set for 75 minutes on HIGH (85 minutes for roasts more than 2 ½ inches thick).

4 PERFORM a quick release to release the cooker's pressure. Add the potatoes, onion, carrots, and celery to the pot, re-secure the cooker's lid, and set for 5 minutes on HIGH.

5 LET the cooker's pressure release naturally 10 minutes before quick releasing any remaining pressure.

6 CAREFULLY transfer roast and vegetables to a serving dish and cover with aluminum foil. Set the cooker to HIGH or "brown" with lid off and whisk the cornstarch and water into the cooking liquid. Let simmer 2 minutes to thicken before stirring in butter. Smother meat and vegetables with the gravy before serving.

Lasagna

Pressure Cooked in Only 6 Minutes

I was at a potluck and was surprised to see that someone brought a slow cooker lasagna that was absolutely delicious. The first thing I thought was... why can't this be done in a pressure cooker? And so I got to the kitchen and created this recipe for what may be the fastest homemade lasagna ever!

SHOPPING LIST

1 tablespoon olive oil

1 yellow onion, diced

1 pound lean ground beef

Salt and pepper

1 (24-ounce) jar chunky spaghetti sauce

¼ cup water

2 pounds whole milk ricotta cheese

2 large eggs

⅓ cup grated Parmesan cheese

2 teaspoons minced garlic

1 teaspoon Italian seasoning

8 ounces uncooked lasagna noodles

1 ½ cups shredded mozzarella cheese

HELPFUL TIP

While cutting slices from the lasagna is easier in large oval cookers, this recipe was tested and successfully prepared in a 4-quart round pressure cooker, so cook away!

1. HEAT olive oil in a large sauté pan on the stove top over HIGH heat. Add onions, ground beef, and a pinch of salt and pepper, sautéing until browned.

2. STIR spaghetti sauce and water into the ground beef mixture, and remove from heat.

3. IN a large mixing bowl, use a fork to whisk together ricotta cheese, eggs, Parmesan cheese, garlic, Italian seasoning, and a pinch of salt and pepper.

4. FILL the bottom of the pressure cooker with water, just until ¼ inch deep. Ladle ⅕ of the beef and sauce mixture into the water and then cover with a layer of lasagna noodles, breaking them to fit.

5. COVER the noodles with a layer of ⅓ of the cheese mixture. Cover the cheese mixture with another layer of ⅕ of the sauce, then another layer of noodles. Repeat for 2 more layers, ending with noodles topped with the final layer of sauce.

6. SECURELY lock the cooker's lid and set for 6 minutes on HIGH. Quick release the cooker's pressure, remove cover, and sprinkle with the mozzarella cheese. Re-cover and let rest at least 10 minutes before serving.

BEEF

German Pot Roast

My Loose Rendition of Sauerbraten

Traditionally, sauerbraten is marinated for as many as ten days, using a vinegary marinade to tenderize the meat. With my German Pot Roast, you get the wonderful textures and flavors in a fraction of the time and effort.

SHOPPING LIST

1 (2- to 3-pound) beef chuck roast

3 tablespoons all-purpose flour

Salt and pepper

2 tablespoons vegetable oil

2 onions, chopped

¾ cup sliced dill pickles

1 cup beef stock or broth

½ cup Dijon mustard

¼ cup dry red wine

2 tablespoons light brown sugar

1 tablespoon minced garlic

2 bay leaves

¼ teaspoon ground allspice

1 tablespoon cornstarch, mixed into 2 tablespoons water

3 tablespoons butter or margarine

MAKE IT YOURS

The red wine in this recipe can be replaced with 2 teaspoons cider vinegar, if desired.

1 SPRINKLE the chuck roast with flour that has been generously seasoned with salt and pepper.

2 WITH the cooker's lid off, heat oil on HIGH or "brown," until sizzling. Place the floured roast in the cooker and brown on each side.

3 ADD the onions, pickles, beef stock, mustard, wine, brown sugar, garlic, bay leaves, and allspice to the cooker. Securely lock the pressure cooker's lid and set for 80 minutes on HIGH (90 minutes for roasts more than 2 ½ inches thick).

4 LET the cooker's pressure release naturally for 10 minutes before quick releasing any remaining pressure.

5 CAREFULLY transfer roast to a serving dish and cover with aluminum foil. Set the cooker to HIGH or "brown" with lid off, and whisk the cornstarch mixture into the cooking liquid. Let simmer 2 minutes to thicken before stirring in butter. Smother meat with the gravy before serving.

BEEF

Prep Time	Cook Time	Temperature	Serves
5 min	80 min	High	6

Honey Mustard Corned Beef

A New and Unique Twist on Corned Beef

Most people simply prepare the traditional boiled corned beef with root vegetables, but I find that corned beef can be a lot more versatile than you would think. This recipe smothers it in a sweet and tangy glaze that you place under the broiler to lightly brown just before serving.

SHOPPING LIST

1 flat cut corned beef (about 3-pounds) with pickling spice packet

1 tablespoon minced garlic

¼ cup whole-grain mustard

2 tablespoons honey

1 tablespoon light brown sugar

MAKE IT A MEAL

This Honey Mustard Corned Beef goes extremely well with simple roasted potatoes. See my Rosemary Pot Roast recipe (page: 50) for a quick version of roasted potatoes. To prepare both at the same time, simply bake the corned beef along with the potatoes for 10–12 minutes instead of broiling.

1 DRAIN and rinse corned beef and place in pressure cooker. Fill pressure cooker pot with just enough water to cover the meat.

2 EMPTY contents of the pickling spice packet into the pot, securely lock the cooker's lid, and set for 80 minutes on HIGH for a 3-pound corned beef (95 minutes for 4 pounds).

3 LET the pressure cooker's pressure release naturally for 10 minutes before performing a quick release to release any remaining pressure.

4 PLACE oven rack in the second-highest position and preheat broiler to HIGH. Transfer corned beef to a sheet pan.

5 COMBINE minced garlic, mustard, honey, and brown sugar to create a glaze. Spread the glaze equally over the surface of the corned beef.

6 PLACE sheet pan under broiler and broil 5–8 minutes, or until glaze is beginning to brown. Let rest 5 minutes before carving.

Layered Enchilada Casserole

Beef Enchiladas, Simplified

Enchiladas may be the ultimate southwestern dish of the century—an epic amount of cheese and salsa and corn tortilla goodness, though this version is done in only five minutes under pressure.

SHOPPING LIST

1 tablespoon olive oil

1 red onion, diced

1 pound lean ground beef

Salt and pepper

1 (16-ounce) jar chunky salsa

1 (4-ounce) can chopped green chiles, drained

2 tomatoes, diced

½ cup sliced black olives

1 tablespoon chopped fresh cilantro

12 (6-inch) soft corn tortillas

1 ½ cups shredded Mexican cheese blend

Sour cream

MAKE IT YOURS

Try substituting a jar of salsa verde in place of the regular salsa for a somewhat more traditional take on enchiladas.

1 HEAT oil in a large sauté pan on the stove top over HIGH heat. Add onion, ground beef, and a pinch of salt and pepper, sautéing until browned.

2 STIR salsa, green chiles, tomatoes, olives, and cilantro into the ground beef mixture, and remove from heat.

3 FILL the bottom of the pressure cooker with water, just until ¼ inch deep. Ladle ⅕ of the beef and salsa mixture into the water, and then cover with a layer of 3 tortillas, overlapping them to fit.

4 COVER the tortillas with another layer of ⅕ of the beef mixture. Create another layer of tortillas. Repeat for 2 more layers, ending with tortillas topped with the final layer of beef mixture.

5 SECURELY lock the cooker's lid and set for 5 minutes on HIGH.

6 QUICK release the cooker's pressure, remove cover, and sprinkle with the cheese. Recover and let rest at least 10 minutes before serving topped with dollops of sour cream.

BEEF

Meatloaf

What You Know and Love, Just Rounded

Meatloaf may be one of the last things you'd expect to cook in a pressure cooker, but I assure you that the results are moist and delicious.

SHOPPING LIST

2 pounds lean ground beef

½ cup Italian bread crumbs

¼ cup grated Parmesan cheese

¼ cup finely minced yellow onion

1 large egg, beaten

1 tablespoon minced garlic

2 teaspoons Worcestershire sauce

½ teaspoon dried thyme

1 teaspoon salt

½ teaspoon pepper

1 tablespoon vegetable oil

1 yellow onion, diced

1 cup ketchup

½ cup beef stock or broth

1 In a large mixing bowl, combine ground beef, bread crumbs, Parmesan cheese, onion, egg, garlic, Worcestershire sauce, thyme, salt, and pepper. Form the mixture into a round loaf, small enough to fit into your pressure cooker.

2 With the cooker's lid off, heat oil on HIGH or "brown," until sizzling.

3 Place onion in the cooker and sauté until translucent, 4–5 minutes.

4 Stir in ketchup and beef stock, and top with the rounded meatloaf. Securely lock the pressure cooker's lid and set for 15 minutes on HIGH.

5 Let the cooker's pressure release naturally for 10 minutes before quick releasing any remaining pressure. Serve topped with sauce from the cooker.

MAKE IT YOURS

For a tangier sauce, try substituting barbecue sauce in place of the ketchup.

BEEF

BEEF

Rosemary Pot Roast

with Roasted Potatoes

This recipe is a great example of how pressure cookers allow you to multitask in the kitchen. With a pressure cooker freeing up your oven, you can roast potatoes at a temperature you would never bake a pot roast.

SHOPPING LIST

1 (2- to 3-pound) beef chuck roast

3 tablespoons all-purpose flour

Salt and pepper

2 tablespoons olive oil

1 yellow onion, diced

1 tablespoon minced garlic

2 cups vegetable stock or broth

1 cup dry red wine (may substitute beef stock)

1 bay leaf

5 sprigs fresh rosemary

1 teaspoon cornstarch, whisked into 1 tablespoon water

2 tablespoons Dijon mustard

3 tablespoons butter or margarine

POTATOES

5 large potatoes, cubed

2 tablespoons olive oil

1 tablespoon Italian seasoning

½ teaspoon garlic powder

MAKE IT MEMORABLE

While it is best to remove the cooked sprigs of rosemary before serving, placing fresh, green sprigs on the serving platter makes for a very nice presentation.

1 SPRINKLE the chuck roast with flour that has been generously seasoned with salt and pepper. With the cooker's lid off, heat oil on HIGH or "brown," until sizzling. Place the floured roast in the cooker and brown on each side.

2 ADD the onion, garlic, vegetable stock, red wine, bay leaf, rosemary, and a pinch of salt and pepper to the cooker. Securely lock the cooker's lid and set for 75 minutes on HIGH (85 for roasts more than 2 ½ inches thick).

3 WHEN the roast is nearly finished cooking, prepare the potatoes by preheating an oven to 475°. In a large bowl, toss all potato ingredients, as well as a pinch of salt and pepper together.

4 SPREAD the coated potatoes on a large sheet pan and bake 20–25 minutes, shaking the pan every few minutes until potatoes are browned on most sides.

5 LET the cooker's pressure release naturally before removing roast to rest under aluminum foil. Strain off 1 cup of the cooking liquid and discard. Set the cooker to HIGH with lid off and whisk the cornstarch and water, Dijon mustard, and butter into the remaining cooking liquid. Let simmer 2 minutes to thicken before serving over the roast and roasted potatoes.

Cheeseburger Macaroni

A Stove-Top Favorite, Made Off the Stove

With this American classic, you get the best of both worlds—pasta and cheeseburgers, done quick and chock-full of flavor. It's sure to warm your spirits as well as your belly.

SHOPPING LIST

1 tablespoon vegetable oil

1 pound lean ground beef

1 small yellow onion, diced

½ teaspoon salt

¼ teaspoon pepper

½ teaspoon dry thyme

¼ cup ketchup

3 cups elbow macaroni

3 cups beef stock or broth

12 ounces processed cheese (like Velveeta)

1 WITH the cooker's lid off, heat oil on HIGH or "brown," until sizzling. Place the ground beef in the cooker, and cook until browned.

2 ADD remaining ingredients, except for the cheese, to the cooker.

3 SECURELY lock the pressure cooker's lid and set for 6 minutes on HIGH.

4 PERFORM a quick release to release the cooker's pressure.

5 ADD the processed cheese, stirring until melted and creamy. Let sit 5 minutes to thicken before serving.

CUT THE FAT

Ground turkey breast can be used in place of the ground beef, and 2% processed cheese can be used in place of the regular processed cheese to dramatically cut the fat in this recipe.

Chuck Wagon Beef Stew

with Biscuit Dumplings

Robust flavors and filling ingredients set this beef stew apart from the soup world. There is no confusion here—this is a meal in a bowl.

SHOPPING LIST

2 tablespoons vegetable oil

2 pounds stew meat, cubed

Salt and pepper

1 large red onion, chopped

1 tablespoon minced garlic

1 tablespoon chili powder

1 teaspoon cumin

1 green bell pepper, chopped

1 red bell pepper, chopped

1 (15-ounce) can diced tomatoes, with juice

3 ½ cups beef stock or broth

1 tablespoon chopped fresh cilantro

1 (15-ounce) can pinto beans, drained → RANCH BEANS c̄ SAUCE

1 cup whole-kernel corn

2 tablespoons cornmeal starch c̄ H₂O

1 (6- to 8-ounce) can refrigerated biscuits

1 WITH the cooker's lid off, heat oil on HIGH or "brown," until sizzling.

2 SEASON stew meat with a generous amount of salt and pepper, place in the cooker, and sauté until lightly browned.

3 ADD onion, garlic, chili powder, cumin, green bell pepper, red bell pepper, tomatoes, beef stock, and cilantro. Securely lock the pressure cooker's lid and set for 20 minutes on HIGH.

4 PERFORM a quick release to release the cooker's pressure. With the cooker's lid off, set to HIGH or "brown." Stir in pinto beans and corn and bring to a simmer.

5 STIR in cornmeal, and simmer 2 minutes to thicken. Separate refrigerated biscuits, drop in, and let simmer 10–15 minutes before serving.

HELPFUL TIP

Be sure to stir constantly as you add the cornmeal in the last step, otherwise it may clump together.

Classic Beef Stroganoff

with Chunks of Tender Beef in a Creamy Gravy

Stroganoff, with its creamy mushroom gravy, is one of my all-time favorite dishes. Pressure cooking this classic rendition allows you to get tender chunks of beef in only 15 minutes... the perfect amount of time to boil egg noodles to serve under it.

SHOPPING LIST

2 tablespoons butter or margarine

1 tablespoon vegetable oil

1 ½ pounds sirloin steak, cubed

1 yellow onion, finely diced

8 ounces button mushrooms, quartered

½ cup beef stock or broth

1 tablespoon lemon juice

¼ teaspoon garlic powder

⅛ teaspoon allspice

⅛ teaspoon pepper

8 ounces sour cream

2 tablespoons chopped fresh parsley

¼ teaspoon salt

1 WITH the cooker's lid off, heat butter and oil on HIGH or "brown," until melted and sizzling.

2 PLACE the steak and onion in the cooker, and cook until steak is lightly browned, about 5 minutes.

3 ADD mushrooms, beef stock, lemon juice, garlic powder, allspice, and pepper and securely lock the pressure cooker's lid. Set the cooker for 15 minutes on HIGH.

4 LET the pressure release naturally for 5 minutes before performing a quick release to release any remaining pressure.

5 WITH the cooker off, stir in sour cream, parsley, and salt before serving.

MAKE IT BETTER

For an extra beefy sauce, skip adding the salt in the last step and add beef base to taste instead. Adding more beef base gives the flavor of a reduced gravy without having to actually spend the time to cook it down.

Pizza Joes

A Crowd-Pleasing Twist on Sloppy Joes

This recipe combines two family-favorites—Sloppy Joes and pizza—to make something destined to become a new family favorite. Makes enough to serve on 12 regular-size hamburger buns.

SHOPPING LIST

1 tablespoon vegetable oil

1 pound lean ground beef

1 small yellow onion, diced

¼ teaspoon garlic powder

1 (16-ounce) jar chunky spaghetti sauce

½ cup finely diced green bell pepper

24 slices pepperoni, chopped

12 hamburger buns

Grated Parmesan cheese

1 WITH the cooker's lid off, heat oil on HIGH or "brown," until sizzling.

2 PLACE the ground beef, onion, and garlic powder in the cooker, and cook until ground beef is lightly browned, about 7 minutes.

3 ADD the spaghetti sauce and bell pepper and securely lock the pressure cooker's lid. Set the pressure cooker for 8 minutes on HIGH.

4 PERFORM a quick release to release the cooker's pressure.

5 STIR pepperoni into the Pizza Joe mixture before spooning onto hamburger buns and topping with a generous amount of grated Parmesan cheese.

MAKE IT BETTER

While hamburger buns are more like classic Sloppy Joes, this *Pizza Joe* mixture is even better served open-faced over hot garlic bread.

Salsa Stewed Beef and Rice

A Quick and Easy Southwestern Favorite

This is a really simple all-in-one weekday meal that is great for feeding the whole family. Most of the ingredients are pantry staples too, except the fresh cilantro, but you can leave that out in a pinch.

SHOPPING LIST

1 tablespoon olive oil

1 pound lean ground beef

1 red onion, diced

1 teaspoon chili powder

½ teaspoon salt

1 cup long-grain white rice, rinsed well

2 cups water

1 (16-ounce) jar chunky salsa

1 (15-ounce) can seasoned black beans, drained and rinsed

1 cup frozen corn kernels

2 tablespoons chopped fresh cilantro

1 cup shredded Cheddar cheese

1 WITH the cooker's lid off, heat oil on HIGH or "brown," until sizzling.

2 PLACE the ground beef, onion, chili powder, and salt in the cooker, and cook until ground beef is lightly browned, about 7 minutes.

3 ADD the water, rice, and salsa and securely lock the pressure cooker's lid. Set the pressure cooker for 8 minutes on HIGH.

4 PERFORM a quick release to release the cooker's pressure. Set cooker to HIGH or "brown."

5 STIR black beans, corn, and cilantro into the mixture and cook 3–4 minutes, just until corn is heated throughout. Serve topped with shredded Cheddar cheese.

MAKE IT YOURS

You can also make this with ground turkey or even cubed steak, chicken, or pork. For tender meat without overcooking the rice, cut meats into smaller cubes that are only about ½ inch thick.

Greek Beef Roast

with Creamy Yogurt Gravy

This recipe creates a fork-tender roast in the style of Greek Souvlaki, with creamy dill gravy made from extra-thick Greek yogurt.

BEEF

SHOPPING LIST

1 (2- to 3-pound) beef chuck roast

3 tablespoons all-purpose flour

Salt and pepper

2 tablespoons olive oil

1 yellow onion, diced

2 tablespoons minced garlic

2 cups chicken stock or broth

1 tablespoon lemon juice

1 tablespoon dried oregano

1 teaspoon cornstarch, whisked into 1 tablespoon water

8 ounces plain Greek yogurt

2 teaspoons chopped fresh dill

1 tomato, diced, for garnish

MAKE IT A MEAL

I like to serve this alongside grilled or skillet-fried pita bread to soak up the gravy. Oil and grill thick slices of summer squash and/or eggplant to create a full meal.

1 SPRINKLE the chuck roast with flour that has been generously seasoned with salt and pepper.

2 WITH the cooker's lid off, heat oil on HIGH or "brown," until sizzling. Place the floured roast in the cooker and brown on each side.

3 ADD the onion, garlic, chicken stock, lemon juice, oregano, and a pinch of salt and pepper to the cooker. Securely lock the cooker's lid and set for 60 minutes on HIGH. (75 minutes for roasts more than 2 ½ inches thick.)

4 LET the cooker's pressure release naturally before removing roast to rest under aluminum foil.

5 STRAIN off 1 cup of the cooking liquid and discard. Set the cooker to HIGH or "brown" with lid off and whisk the cornstarch and water into the remaining cooking liquid. Let simmer 2 minutes to thicken before stirring in yogurt and dill. Return meat to the gravy before serving topped with diced tomato.

Two-Can Cola Beef or Pork Roast

A New and Improved Recipe for a Quick and Easy Roast

Even after perfecting one of my favorite ways to prepare a roast, I still haven't quite figured out why two cans of cola make this so delicious. However odd it may sound, it does something magical to the meat.

SHOPPING LIST

1 tablespoon vegetable oil

1 (2- to 3-pound) beef chuck or pork loin roast

¼ teaspoon pepper

2 cans regular cola

1 packet powdered onion soup mix

1 tablespoon cornstarch, mixed into 2 tablespoons water

3 tablespoons butter or margarine

CUT THE SUGAR

Though regular cola adds a nice, subtle sweetness to the gravy, diet cola is still good if you want to cut out the added sugar (however, all sweetness will cook out). On the other hand, using a cola sweetened with Splenda may make the gravy too sweet. (Use only 1 can of this and 1 can water.)

1 WITH the cooker's lid off, heat oil on HIGH or "brown," until sizzling. Season the beef or pork loin with pepper, place in cooker, and brown on each side.

2 ADD cola and onion soup mix, securely lock the cooker's lid, and set for 60 minutes on HIGH (75 minutes for roasts more than 3 inches thick).

3 LET the cooker's pressure release naturally before removing roast to rest under aluminum foil.

4 STRAIN off 1 cup of the cooking liquid and discard. Set the cooker to HIGH or "brown" with lid off and whisk the cornstarch and water into the remaining cooking liquid. Let simmer 2 minutes to thicken before stirring in butter. Carve, and serve meat smothered in the gravy.

BEEF

Corned Beef

with Warm BBQ Apple Slaw

The Warm BBQ Apple Slaw in this recipe is not just a welcome change from bland cabbage, but the perfect savory and sweet side for salty corned beef.

SHOPPING LIST

1 flat cut corned beef (3–4 pounds) with pickling spice packet

1 tablespoon vegetable oil

1 large yellow onion, thinly sliced

1 (16-ounce) bag shredded coleslaw cabbage

⅓ cup cider vinegar

½ cup bold BBQ sauce

1 teaspoon yellow mustard

1 teaspoon light brown sugar

¼ teaspoon salt

⅛ teaspoon pepper

2 large apples, cored and thinly sliced

2 tablespoons butter or margarine

MAKE IT FASTER

The cook times for this recipe are for extra tender corned beef, though you can cut them down by 10 minutes if you prefer the meat to be a little more firm. For cuts of meat that are more than 3 ½ inches thick, adding 10 minutes is recommended.

1 DRAIN and rinse corned beef and place in pressure cooker. Fill pressure cooker pot with just enough water to cover the meat.

2 EMPTY contents of the pickling spice packet into the pot, securely lock the cooker's lid, and set for 80 minutes on HIGH for a 3 pound corned beef (95 minutes for 4 pounds).

3 WHEN there is 30 minutes left on the cooker, heat the oil in a large skillet over medium-high heat. Add the onions and sauté until they begin to caramelize, about 10 minutes.

4 ADD remaining ingredients, except apples and butter, and reduce heat to MEDIUM. Cook for 15 minutes, stirring occasionally.

5 ADD the apples and continue cooking for 10 minutes. Reduce heat to LOW and stir in butter. Keep slaw on the lowest heat until corned beef is ready to serve.

6 LET the pressure cooker's pressure release naturally for 10 minutes before performing a quick release to release any remaining pressure. Transfer corned beef to a carving board and cover with aluminum foil. Let rest 10 minutes before slicing and serving alongside the Warm BBQ Apple Slaw.

Bacon Braised Short Ribs

with Brown Sugar

Braised short ribs are some of the most tender beef you can make, but the process of braising them can take as long as five hours to achieve the same results that this recipe creates in only 35 minutes.

SHOPPING LIST

5 strips bacon

3–4 pounds bone-in short ribs, trimmed of excess fat

Salt and pepper

½ cup diced red onion

1 tablespoon minced garlic

1 cup beef stock or broth

2 teaspoons balsamic vinegar

1 tablespoon light brown sugar

1 teaspoon dried thyme

2 teaspoons cornstarch, whisked into 1 tablespoon water

3 tablespoons butter or margarine

MAKE IT A MEAL

These short ribs and the sauce served along with them go amazingly well with cheese tortellini. You can buy either refrigerated "fresh" tortellini, or even frozen bags of tortellini and prepare it according to the package directions as the short ribs cook.

1 WITH the cooker's lid off, heat bacon on HIGH or "brown," until nearly crisp. Remove bacon, coarsely chop, and set aside.

2 SPRINKLE short ribs with a generous amount of salt and pepper, and add to the bacon grease in the cooker to brown on both sides. (For smaller cookers, do this in multiple batches until all are browned.)

3 ADD chopped bacon and remaining ingredients, except cornstarch and butter, and securely lock the pressure cooker's lid. Set the cooker for 35 minutes on HIGH.

4 LET the pressure release naturally for 10 minutes before performing a quick release for any remaining pressure.

5 TRANSFER the cooked short ribs to a serving platter and set the cooker to HIGH or "brown" until the cooking liquid is simmering. Whisk the cornstarch and water mixture into the liquid and cook 2 minutes, until thickened. Stir in butter and a pinch of salt and pepper before ladling the sauce over the short ribs to serve.

BBQ Beef Tips

Moist and Tender BBQ in Minutes

This recipe is about as simple as barbecue gets! With such tender cuts of beef in a homemade sauce, you'd never believe it was cooked in only 15 minutes. Best served over rice (but mashed potatoes are good too).

SHOPPING LIST

1 tablespoon vegetable oil

1 pound sirloin steak, cubed

1 yellow onion, diced

1 (6-ounce) can tomato paste

¼ cup white vinegar

1 tablespoon yellow mustard

1 tablespoon Worcestershire sauce

3 tablespoons water

2 tablespoons light brown sugar

½ teaspoon garlic powder

½ teaspoon salt

¼ teaspoon pepper

1 WITH the cooker's lid off, heat oil on HIGH or "brown," until sizzling.

2 PLACE the steak and onion in the cooker, and cook until steak is lightly browned, about 5 minutes.

3 ADD remaining ingredients and stir until combined.

4 SECURELY lock the pressure cooker's lid and set for 15 minutes on HIGH.

5 LET the pressure release naturally for 10 minutes before performing a quick release for any remaining pressure.

6 ADD any additional salt and pepper to taste before serving.

MAKE IT EASIER

This can also be made with 1 ¼ cups of your favorite prepared BBQ sauce and ¼ cup water in place of all of the ingredients added in step 3.

POULTRY

Easiest Ever Chicken and Dumplings

Or At Least as Easy as I Could Make It

When it comes to Midwestern and southern cuisine, chicken and dumplings is a widespread staple, usually taking over an hour to prepare. Here, it is simplified, sacrificing absolutely no flavor.

SHOPPING LIST

3 tablespoons butter or margarine

1 ½ pounds boneless, skinless chicken thighs, sliced thick

Salt and pepper

1 yellow onion, diced

6 cups chicken stock or broth

3 ribs celery, sliced

1 ½ cups baby carrots

1 teaspoon dried thyme

½ teaspoon poultry seasoning

¼ teaspoon pepper

1 cup frozen corn kernels, thawed

1 ¾ cups Bisquick baking mix

⅔ cup milk

¼ cup heavy cream

MAKE IT BETTER

Try mixing ¼ cup grated Parmesan cheese into the dumpling mixture in step 6 for even better dumplings.

1 WITH the cooker's lid off, heat butter on HIGH or "brown," until melted and sizzling.

2 GENEROUSLY season chicken with salt and pepper, place in the cooker, and cook until lightly browned, about 5 minutes.

3 ADD in onion, chicken stock, celery, carrots, thyme, poultry seasoning, and pepper. Securely lock the pressure cooker's lid and set for 8 minutes on HIGH.

4 PERFORM a quick release to release the cooker's pressure.

5 WITH the cooker's lid off, set to HIGH or "brown." Add in corn kernels and let simmer.

6 MEANWHILE, whisk together Bisquick baking mix and milk, and drop by the spoonfuls into the pot. Let dumplings simmer for 8–10 minutes.

7 TURN off heat, stir in heavy cream, and add salt to taste.

Bourbon Chicken Thighs

Chicken in a Sweet and Tangy Sauce

Bourbon chicken is a great way to put that bottle of whiskey to use, as the alcohol cooks right out, leaving both its flavor and your wits intact.

SHOPPING LIST

1 tablespoon olive oil

2 pounds boneless, skinless chicken thighs

½ cup chili sauce

⅓ cup apple juice

3 tablespoons soy sauce

1 tablespoon bourbon liquor

1 tablespoon light brown sugar

½ teaspoon onion powder

¼ teaspoon garlic powder

¼ teaspoon crushed red pepper

¼ teaspoon ground ginger

2 teaspoons cornstarch, mixed into 1 tablespoon water

1 WITH the cooker's lid off, heat oil on HIGH or "brown," until sizzling.

2 PLACE chicken thighs in cooker and sauté until browned.

3 ADD chili sauce, apple juice, soy sauce, bourbon, brown sugar, onion powder, garlic powder, crushed red pepper, and ground ginger to the cooker.

4 SECURELY lock the pressure cooker's lid and set for 8 minutes on HIGH.

5 PERFORM a quick release to release the cooker's pressure.

6 WITH the lid off, set the cooker to HIGH or "brown." Stir in cornstarch mixture and let simmer 2 minutes, until sauce is thickened. Serve chicken thighs drizzled in the bourbon sauce.

MAKE IT YOURS

Though the alcohol does cook out, you may still substitute it with 1 tablespoon apple cider vinegar, if desired.

Honey Garlic Chicken

Sun-Kissed and Savory

With honey and garlic being the stars, the classic combination of flavors in this chicken dish makes it special, leaving the possibilities endless when it comes to side dish choices.

POULTRY

SHOPPING LIST

4 boneless, skinless chicken breasts

¼ teaspoon garlic powder

½ teaspoon salt

⅛ teaspoon pepper

3 tablespoons butter or margarine

½ cup chicken stock or broth

2 tablespoons minced garlic

2 tablespoons honey

1 teaspoon soy sauce

MAKE IT YOURS

Light agave nectar can be used in place of the honey as a lower glycemic index option for those watching their sugar intake.

1 Toss chicken breasts with garlic powder, salt, and pepper to combine.

2 WITH the cooker's lid off, heat butter on HIGH or "brown," until melted and sizzling.

3 PLACE seasoned chicken in the cooker, browning on both sides, and then pour in the chicken stock.

4 IN a small bowl or ramekin, combine the minced garlic, honey, and soy sauce. Spread the mixture over top chicken breasts in the cooker.

5 SECURELY lock the pressure cooker's lid and set for 8 minutes on HIGH.

6 PERFORM a quick release to release the cooker's pressure, and then serve immediately.

Chicken with Apples and Bacon

Smothered with Two of the Best Things in the World

Apples and bacon are two foods that were simply meant to find their way into dishes like this one! The sweet and slightly acidic apples complement the salty and smoky bacon in the most wonderful way. For something even better, try topping with shredded sharp Cheddar cheese just before serving!

SHOPPING LIST

4 strips thick-cut bacon

4 boneless, skinless chicken breasts

3 tablespoons butter or margarine

1 yellow onion, thinly sliced

8 leaves fresh sage, chopped

3 apples, peeled, cored and cut into 8 wedges

½ cup apple juice

2 tablespoons Dijon mustard

1 tablespoon light brown sugar

¼ teaspoon salt

⅛ teaspoon pepper

CUT THE FAT

To make a lower fat version of this dish you can simply substitute turkey bacon for the regular bacon in step 1 and use Smart Balance Light or another similar light margarine in place of the butter in step 3.

POULTRY

1 WITH the cooker's lid off, heat bacon on HIGH or "brown," until crisp. Remove from cooker, crumble, and set aside.

2 PLACE chicken breasts in cooker and brown in the bacon fat on both sides. Remove browned chicken from cooker and set aside.

3 PLACE butter and onion in the cooker, and cook just until onion becomes translucent, 3–4 minutes.

4 RETURN chicken and crumbled bacon to the cooker and cover with remaining ingredients, stirring to combine.

5 SECURELY lock the pressure cooker's lid and set for 8 minutes on HIGH.

6 PERFORM a quick release to release the cooker's pressure. Serve each chicken breast smothered with a heaping spoonful of the apple, onion, and bacon mixture.

Chicken Leg Quarters

with Lemon and Rosemary

This surprisingly humble, light-tasting chicken recipe is perfect for an end of day meal—the kind of dish you quite simply throw into a pot and do not even worry about until it's done.

POULTRY

SHOPPING LIST

2 ½ pounds chicken leg quarters, skin removed

½ cup chicken stock or broth

3 tablespoons butter or margarine

Juice of 1 lemon

1 tablespoon minced garlic

1 ½ teaspoons dried rosemary

1 teaspoon lemon zest

1 teaspoon sugar

¼ teaspoon dried thyme

¾ teaspoon salt

¼ teaspoon pepper

1 ADD all ingredients to the cooker.

2 SECURELY lock the pressure cooker's lid and set for 14 minutes on HIGH.

3 LET the cooker's pressure release naturally for 10 minutes before quick releasing any remaining pressure.

4 SERVE immediately.

MAKE IT YOURS

This classic combination of flavors works well with any cut of chicken. Use any that you wish, and cook according to the cook time reference at the back of this book.

Shredded Chicken Tacos

A Simple Weekday Staple

This recipe for tacos with chicken pulled right into the sauce will surely have your taste buds jumping like beans.

POULTRY

SHOPPING LIST

1 tablespoon vegetable oil

1 red onion, diced

1 red bell pepper, diced

1 jalapeño pepper, seeded and finely diced

Juice of 1 lime

1 tablespoon chili powder

1 tablespoon light brown sugar

½ teaspoon salt

1 (16-ounce) jar chunky salsa

¾ cup chicken stock or broth

2 pounds boneless, skinless chicken breasts

Soft flour or hard corn taco shells

Shredded lettuce

3 tomatoes, diced

8 ounces shredded Cheddar-Jack cheese

1 WITH the cooker's lid off, heat oil on HIGH or "brown," until sizzling.

2 PLACE onion, bell pepper, and jalapeño pepper in the sizzling butter, and sauté until onion is translucent.

3 ADD the lime juice, chili powder, brown sugar, salt, salsa, and chicken stock to the onion concoction, and stir together.

4 ADD chicken breasts to the cooker, securely lock the pressure cooker's lid, and set for 12 minutes on HIGH.

5 LET the pressure cooker's pressure release naturally for 15 minutes before performing a quick release to release any remaining pressure.

6 USING a fork, shred cooked chicken into the sauce in the cooker.

7 ASSEMBLE tacos by filling taco shells with lettuce, tomatoes, Cheddar-Jack cheese, and shredded chicken.

MAKE IT YOURS

Feel free to make this pulled chicken meat into burritos as well. Simply roll the chicken, rice, beans, cheese, or any of your favorite Mexicans staples into a flour tortilla.

Stuffed Chicken Breasts

with Roasted Red Peppers, Kalamata Olives, and Feta

There simply isn't any other way to get all these flavors without a little bit of arm movement. The real beauty of this dish, stuffed with a few of my favorite Greek ingredients, is that it delivers all it has to offer in every single bite.

POULTRY

SHOPPING LIST

4 boneless, skinless chicken breasts

Salt, pepper, and Italian seasoning

½ cup sliced roasted red peppers

¼ cup kalamata olives, roughly chopped

1 tablespoon chopped fresh oregano

1 tablespoon olive oil

⅔ cup chicken stock or broth

½ cup crumbled feta cheese

MAKE IT A MEAL

Serve with a side of couscous and a quick sauté of zucchini and squash with a pinch of dried oregano for a full Greek meal.

1 LAY chicken breasts between 2 plastic wrap sheets, and use a meat mallet or rolling pin to pound down until about ⅓ inch thick.

2 GENEROUSLY season both sides of the flattened chicken with salt, pepper, and Italian seasoning.

3 COMBINE peppers, olives, and oregano, and place on top of seasoned chicken. Roll up, and secure chicken with toothpicks.

4 WITH the cooker's lid off, heat oil on HIGH or "brown," until sizzling. Add the stuffed chicken and cook until lightly browned on both sides, about 5 minutes.

5 ADD chicken stock, securely lock the pressure cooker's lid, and set for 8 minutes on HIGH.

6 PERFORM a quick release to release the cooker's pressure. Serve stuffed chicken breasts topped with feta cheese.

The Whole Bird

Falling-Off-The-Bone Tender

There may be no better way to cook chicken than whole, full of its own juices and tender as can be! With this recipe for whole chicken, I highly suggest using the white wine (although it is optional), as it adds a sweet contrast to the lemon.

POULTRY

SHOPPING LIST

1 teaspoon paprika

¼ teaspoon dried thyme

¼ teaspoon poultry seasoning

½ teaspoon salt

¼ teaspoon pepper

1 (3- to 4-) pound whole chicken, rinsed well

2 tablespoons olive oil

1 ½ cups chicken stock or broth

2 tablespoons dry white wine, optional

Juice of 1 lemon

PLAY IT SAFE

Be careful when transferring this chicken from the cooker, as it is truly so moist that the wings and legs may simply fall right off!

1 IN a small bowl or ramekin, combine the paprika, thyme, poultry seasoning, salt, and pepper. Rub the mixture into the entire surface of the chicken.

2 WITH the cooker's lid off, heat oil on HIGH or "brown," until sizzling.

3 PLACE chicken in cooker, breast side down, and let cook until browned, about 7 minutes.

4 FLIP the chicken in the cooker, and cover with remaining ingredients.

5 SECURELY lock the pressure cooker's lid and set for 25 minutes on HIGH.

6 LET the cooker's pressure release naturally for 10 minutes before performing a quick release to release any remaining pressure.

7 REMOVE from cooker, and let rest 5 minutes before pulling apart and carving. Serve drizzled with juices from the cooker.

Chicken Fricassee

with White Wine and Mushrooms

This take on the classic dish with many interpretations combines chicken with the complementary flavors of mushrooms, celery, zesty lemon, and white wine in a creamy sauce.

SHOPPING LIST

4 boneless, skinless chicken breasts

2 tablespoons all-purpose flour

Salt and pepper

2 tablespoons butter or margarine

1 yellow onion, thinly sliced

8 ounces button mushrooms, halved

½ cup chopped celery

1 tablespoon minced garlic

1 ½ cups chicken stock or broth

¼ cup dry white wine

1 teaspoon lemon zest

½ teaspoon poultry seasoning

1 tablespoon cornstarch, mixed into 1 tablespoon water

1 cup sour cream

3 tablespoons chopped fresh parsley

MAKE IT YOURS

Though the alcohol cooks out, the wine in this recipe can be replaced with the juice of 1 lemon, if desired.

1 Toss chicken in flour that has been generously seasoned with salt and pepper, until each breast is lightly coated.

2 With the cooker's lid off, heat butter on HIGH or "brown," until melted and sizzling. Place chicken breasts in cooker, and sauté until lightly browned, about 5 minutes.

3 Add onion, mushrooms, celery, garlic, chicken stock, wine, lemon zest, and poultry seasoning. Securely lock the pressure cooker's lid and set for 8 minutes on HIGH.

4 Perform a quick release to release the cooker's pressure.

5 With the cooker's lid off, set to HIGH or "brown." Stir in cornstarch mixture, and simmer for 2 minutes, or until sauce is thickened.

6 Turn off heat, and stir in sour cream. Top with fresh parsley, and season with salt and pepper to taste before serving.

POULTRY

Pizza Style Chicken Breasts

with Pepperoni and Mozzarella Cheese

This recipe is a simple and quick way to prepare a meal that is sure to please the whole family. Boil spaghetti on the stove as you prep and pressure cook the chicken for a complete dinner in just 30 minutes!

SHOPPING LIST

4 boneless, skinless chicken breasts

¼ cup all-purpose flour

Salt and pepper

2 tablespoons olive oil

1 (24-ounce) jar chunky spaghetti sauce

1 small green bell pepper, diced

2 tablespoons water

24 slices pepperoni

1 cup shredded mozzarella cheese

MAKE IT FASTER

You can also make this by simply stirring the pepperoni into the sauce after removing the lid in step 5. Then serve topped with a generous amount of grated Parmesan cheese instead of the mozzarella to skip the broiling step altogether.

1 Toss the chicken breasts in flour that has been generously seasoned with salt and pepper, until both sides of each are lightly coated.

2 WITH the cooker's lid off, heat oil on HIGH or "brown," until sizzling.

3 PLACE the coated chicken in the cooker, and lightly brown on each side.

4 COVER with spaghetti sauce, bell pepper, and water. Securely lock the pressure cooker's lid and set for 8 minutes on HIGH.

5 PERFORM a quick release to release the cooker's pressure. Place oven rack in its highest position, and set broiler to HIGH.

6 TRANSFER chicken breasts from the cooker to a sheet pan. Spoon a small spoonful of the sauce from the cooker over top each piece, then top each with 6 slices of pepperoni and ¼ of the cheese.

7 PLACE sheet pan under broiler, and broil 3–5 minutes, or until cheese is bubbling and beginning to brown. Serve with additional sauce from the cooker.

Cheesy Chicken and Rice

with Broccoli Florets

This one-pot meal is similar to a casserole, combining a satisfying amount of protein-rich chicken, filling rice, healthy broccoli, and deliciously sharp and creamy Cheddar cheese with very little effort.

SHOPPING LIST

1 tablespoon vegetable oil

1 pound boneless, skinless chicken breasts, cubed

1 yellow onion, diced

1 ⅓ cups long-grain white rice, rinsed well

2 ½ cups chicken stock or broth

¾ teaspoon salt

¼ teaspoon pepper

¼ teaspoon garlic powder

1 ½ tablespoons all-purpose flour

½ cup milk

1 ½ cups shredded Cheddar cheese

2 cups frozen broccoli florets, thawed

1 WITH the cooker's lid off, heat oil on HIGH or "brown," until sizzling. Add the chicken and onion, and sauté until chicken is lightly browned and onion is translucent, about 5 minutes.

2 ADD rice, chicken stock, salt, pepper, and garlic powder, securely lock the pressure cooker's lid, and set for 5 minutes on HIGH.

3 PERFORM a quick release to release the cooker's pressure.

4 WITH the cooker's lid off, set to HIGH or "brown." Whisk together flour and milk, add to the cooker, and simmer for 2 minutes.

5 STIR in Cheddar cheese and broccoli florets, and let simmer for 2 minutes, or until cheese is melted and broccoli is warmed throughout. Serve immediately.

MAKE IT BETTER

Try topping the finished dish with crumbled crackers or toasted almonds for the full casserole experience!

Sweet Onion Teriyaki Chicken

An Irresistible Family Favorite

This quick and delicious Asian entrée is best served over white rice. A word of warning though—with only eight minutes of cooking time under pressure—you are definitely going to want to buy instant rice to prepare alongside this!

SHOPPING LIST

2 tablespoons vegetable oil

2 large yellow onions, thinly sliced

4 boneless, skinless chicken breasts

⅓ cup reduced-sodium teriyaki sauce

¼ cup chicken stock or broth

1 tablespoon minced garlic

½ teaspoon onion powder

1 ½ tablespoons light brown sugar

1 teaspoon cornstarch

2 tablespoons water

MAKE IT BETTER

For an even better result, remove chicken from the thickened sauce and place on the top rack under your oven's broiler to brown before serving. This should only take a minute or two and adds a real nice flavor to the chicken.

1 WITH the cooker's lid off, heat oil on HIGH or "brown," until sizzling.

2 PLACE onions in the cooker, and cook until they begin to caramelize, about 8 minutes.

3 COVER with chicken, teriyaki sauce, chicken stock, garlic, and onion powder and toss to fully coat all.

4 SECURELY lock the pressure cooker's lid and set for 8 minutes on HIGH.

5 PERFORM a quick release to release the cooker's pressure. Remove lid and set cooker to HIGH or "brown."

6 WHISK brown sugar and cornstarch into the 2 tablespoons of water and add to the cooker, stirring into the sauce. Let simmer 2 minutes to thicken.

7 SERVE each chicken breast smothered with a heaping spoonful of the onions and sauce.

Perfected Honey Dijon Chicken

A New and Improved Family-Favorite

Honey mustard chicken is a favorite amongst people of all ages. My new and improved recipe is even more flavorful than before, yet still cooked in only eight minutes.

SHOPPING LIST

2 pounds boneless, skinless chicken breasts or thighs

¼ cup Dijon mustard

¼ cup coarse (whole-grain) mustard

3 tablespoons honey

2 tablespoons light brown sugar

½ teaspoon salt

¼ teaspoon onion powder

1 cup chicken stock or broth

MAKE IT BETTER

For even more flavor, place the re-glazed chicken under a pre-heated broiler set to HIGH for 2–3 minutes, to brown before serving.

1 PLACE chicken at the bottom of the pressure cooker.

2 WHISK together Dijon mustard, coarse mustard, honey, brown sugar, salt, and onion powder to create a Honey Dijon Glaze.

3 SPREAD half of the Honey Dijon Glaze over the chicken in the pressure cooker. Reserve the remaining glaze.

4 POUR chicken broth into cooker, securely lock the pressure cooker's lid, and set to 8 minutes on HIGH.

5 LET the cooker's pressure release naturally 10 minutes before quick releasing any remaining pressure.

6 USE tongs to remove chicken from liquid in the cooker. Spread with remaining Honey Dijon Glaze before serving.

Five-Spiced Chicken

with Tender Sweet Potatoes

If you cannot find it in the spice aisle, the five-spice powder in this recipe is usually available in the Asian foods section of your local grocery store. A fragrant combination of cinnamon, star anise, cloves, fennel, and Szechuan pepper—five-spice powder makes the perfect foil for the tender sweet potatoes cooked right underneath the chicken.

SHOPPING LIST

4 boneless, skinless chicken breasts

3 tablespoons soy sauce

1 teaspoon five-spice powder

¼ teaspoon garlic powder

3 tablespoons butter or margarine

3 sweet potatoes, cut into thick 1-inch cubes

½ cup chicken stock or broth

2 teaspoons honey

MAKE IT A MEAL

While the chicken and sweet potatoes are cooking in the pressure cooker, steam or boil 12 ounces of fresh snap peas for 4–5 minutes, just until crisp-tender. Toss with 1 tablespoon of butter, 1 teaspoon minced garlic, ⅛ teaspoon salt, and the zest of ½ lemon before serving.

1 Toss chicken breasts in soy sauce, five-spice powder, and garlic powder to create a quick marinade. For best flavor, cover and refrigerate at least 1 hour.

2 With the cooker's lid off, heat butter on HIGH or "brown," until melted and sizzling.

3 Remove chicken from marinade (reserving any remaining marinade), and place in cooker, browning on both sides. Remove browned chicken from cooker and set aside.

4 Place cubed sweet potatoes and chicken stock into cooker and drizzle with the reserved marinade.

5 Top sweet potatoes with the browned chicken breasts, and then drizzle each chicken breast with ½ teaspoon of honey.

6 Securely lock the pressure cooker's lid and set for 8 minutes on HIGH.

7 Perform a quick release to release the cooker's pressure. Serve each chicken breast with a heaping spoonful of the sweet potatoes.

POULTRY

Buffalo Chicken Strips

with Crumbled Gorgonzola Cheese

You can't beat the heat when it comes to Buffalo Chicken. There's just something so satisfying about the way blue cheese seems to calm that tingling tongue.

SHOPPING LIST

2 pounds boneless, skinless chicken breasts, cut into thick strips

3 tablespoons all-purpose flour

Salt and pepper

6 tablespoons butter or margarine

1 ½ tablespoons Louisiana Hot Sauce

¼ cup chicken stock or broth

1 teaspoon cornstarch, mixed into 1 tablespoon water

½ cup crumbled Gorgonzola cheese

MAKE IT YOURS

For a more mild sauce, simply cut the hot sauce down to 2 teaspoons. Or for something spicier, simply add more hot sauce to taste before serving. If you've already added the hot sauce and find it too spicy, simply cut it by adding more butter to tone down the heat.

1 TOSS chicken breast strips in flour that has been generously seasoned with salt and pepper, coating well.

2 WITH the cooker's lid off, heat butter on HIGH or "brown," until melted and sizzling.

3 PLACE coated chicken strips in the cooker, and sauté until browned on both sides.

4 ADD hot sauce and chicken stock over top the chicken in the cooker. Securely lock the pressure cooker's lid and set for 6 minutes on HIGH.

5 PERFORM a quick release to release the cooker's pressure.

6 WITH the cooker's lid off, set to HIGH or "brown." Stir in cornstarch mixture, and simmer for 2 minutes, or until sauce has thickened.

7 SERVE chicken strips sprinkled with the Gorgonzola cheese crumbles.

Prep Time	Cook Time	Temperature	Serves
10 min	12 min	High	6

Moist and Tender BBQ Chicken

Off the Grill Taste, Any Time of Year

This recipe pays homage to one of my favorite ways to spend my weekends. Guests wouldn't even know it was done in a pressure cooker!

POULTRY

SHOPPING LIST

2 tablespoons vegetable oil

3 pounds chicken breasts, thighs, and drumsticks

Salt and pepper

1 cup chicken stock or broth

1 tablespoon cider vinegar

1 tablespoon light brown sugar

1 (16-ounce) bottle barbecue sauce

MAKE IT BETTER

Instead of broiling, these are even better when grilled on a preheated grill for 5–7 minutes.

1. WITH the cooker's lid off, heat oil on HIGH or "brown," until sizzling.

2. GENEROUSLY season the chicken with salt and pepper, and then place in the pressure cooker, letting cook until browned on each side.

3. ADD chicken stock, cider vinegar, brown sugar, and ½ of the bottle of barbecue sauce.

4. SECURELY lock the cooker's lid and set for 12 minutes on HIGH.

5. LET the pressure cooker's pressure release naturally for 10 minutes before performing a quick release to release any remaining pressure.

6. TRANSFER chicken to a sheet pan, and spread the remaining barbecue sauce equally over each piece.

7. PLACE sheet pan under broiler and broil 5 minutes, or until sauce is beginning to char. Serve immediately.

PORK

Pork Loin Roast

with Cherry Dijon Sauce

This recipe makes great use of time management by having you prepare the Cherry Dijon Sauce on the stove as the roast is cooking under pressure. There's no need to worry whether cherries are in season either, as frozen cherries work wonderfully.

SHOPPING LIST

1 tablespoon vegetable oil

1 (2- to 3 ½-pound) pork loin roast

Salt and pepper

1 cup chicken stock or broth

1 tablespoon minced garlic

2 teaspoons lemon zest

1 ½ cups frozen cherries

½ cup water

¼ cup Dijon mustard

2 tablespoons light brown sugar

2 teaspoons cornstarch, mixed into 1 tablespoon water

1 tablespoon butter or margarine

HELPFUL TIP

A potato masher will make easy work of mashing the cherries into the Cherry Dijon Sauce. For a completely smooth sauce, a hand blender will get the job done.

1 WITH the cooker's lid off, heat oil on HIGH or "brown," until sizzling.

2 GENEROUSLY season the roast with salt and pepper, place in the cooker, and brown on each side.

3 ADD the chicken stock, garlic, and lemon zest to the cooker and securely lock the cooker's lid. Set for 45 minutes on HIGH.

4 MEANWHILE, create the Cherry Dijon Sauce by placing the frozen cherries, water, Dijon mustard, and light brown sugar in a sauce pot over medium heat. Cover, bring up to a simmer, and let cook 10 minutes.

5 USE a heavy spoon to mash most of the cherries into the sauce before adding cornstarch mixture and letting simmer an additional 3 minutes. Remove from heat and stir in butter.

6 LET the cooker's pressure release naturally 10 minutes before quick releasing any remaining pressure. Remove roast and let rest under aluminum foil 10 minutes before carving and serving smothered in the Cherry Dijon Sauce.

PORK

Moo Shu Pork

Chinese Pork and Cabbage Wraps

This version of the Chinese take-out classic packs most of the traditional flavors in a lot less time than it would take to wait for the delivery guy.

SHOPPING LIST

2 tablespoons sesame oil

1 pound boneless pork loin chops, cut into strips

1 large yellow onion, thinly sliced

1 (16-ounce bag) shredded coleslaw mix

1 tablespoon minced garlic

¼ cup beef stock or broth

3 tablespoons reduced-sodium soy sauce

⅓ cup hoisin sauce

4 scallions, thinly sliced

2 tablespoons cornstarch, mixed into 2 tablespoons water

Flour tortillas

1 WITH the cooker's lid off, heat oil on HIGH or "brown," until sizzling.

2 PLACE the pork and onion in the cooker, and cook until pork is lightly browned, about 5 minutes.

3 ADD the coleslaw mix, garlic, beef broth, and soy sauce, securely lock the pressure cooker's lid, and set for 3 minutes on HIGH.

4 PERFORM a quick release to release the cooker's pressure. Remove lid and set cooker to HIGH or "brown."

5 STIR in hoisin sauce, scallions, and cornstarch mixture. Let simmer 2 minutes.

6 SERVE wrapped in tortillas, spread with additional hoisin sauce, if desired.

HELPFUL TIP

Hoisin, a sweet and smoky Chinese plum sauce, can be found in jars in the Asian foods section of your local grocery store.

PORK

Prep Time	Cook Time	Temperature	Serves
10 min	100 min	High	8

Perfected Pulled Pork

My New and Improved Recipe for Pulled Pork

Smoking pulled pork can take up to 18 hours and constant monitoring to perfect. My new and improved recipe cuts the time immensely and the monitoring altogether.

SHOPPING LIST

1 (4- to 5-pound) pork shoulder or butt

2 tablespoons light brown sugar

1 tablespoon chili powder

2 teaspoons paprika

2 teaspoons salt

1 teaspoon pepper

1 teaspoon dry mustard

1 tablespoon vegetable oil

1 ½ cups chicken stock or broth

2 tablespoons cider vinegar

1 teaspoon liquid smoke

1 (16-ounce) bottle prepared barbecue sauce

MAKE IT YOURS

As pulled pork is traditionally smoked, doubling the amount of liquid smoke will help achieve that same smokehouse flavor. To go even more traditional, skip the last step and serve the pulled pork with sauce on the side.

1 CUT pork into 2-inch thick slices (to speed up the cooking process).

2 COMBINE brown sugar, chili powder, paprika, salt, pepper, and mustard to create a dry rub. Rub onto the surface of all cuts of pork.

3 WITH the cooker's lid off, heat oil on HIGH or "brown," until sizzling. Place the rubbed pork in the cooker and brown on each side.

4 ADD chicken broth, vinegar, and liquid smoke to the cooker, securely lock the pressure cooker's lid, and set for 100 minutes on HIGH.

5 LET the cooker's pressure release naturally 15 minutes before quick releasing any remaining pressure.

6 USING tongs, remove pork from the cooker and then drain all liquid.

7 WITH the cooker's lid off, heat barbecue sauce on HIGH or "brown," until simmering. Pull or shred pork into the simmering sauce before serving.

Sausage and Ricotta Ragu

You'd Swear It Simmered All Day

This robust, sausage-filled Ragu is turned into a "blush" sauce in the last step when you stir in ricotta cheese. I find that this is best served with large, tubular pasta shapes like penne or ziti.

SHOPPING LIST

2 tablespoons olive oil

1 pound ground Italian sausage

1 small yellow onion, diced

2 carrots, diced

2 (15-ounce) cans diced tomatoes

1 (15-ounce) can tomato sauce

2 tablespoons tomato paste

2 teaspoons Italian seasoning

2 teaspoons balsamic vinegar

1 teaspoon sugar

¼ teaspoon crushed red pepper flakes

½ teaspoon salt

8 ounces part-skim ricotta cheese

1 WITH the cooker's lid off, heat oil on HIGH or "brown," until sizzling.

2 PLACE the sausage, onion, and carrots in the cooker, and sauté until sausage has browned, 5–7 minutes.

3 STIR in remaining ingredients, except ricotta cheese, and securely lock the pressure cooker's lid. Set for 10 minutes on HIGH.

4 LET the pressure release naturally for 10 minutes before performing a quick release to release any remaining pressure.

5 WITH the cooker's lid off, set to HIGH or "brown," and stir in ricotta cheese before serving over pasta.

PORK

MAKE IT A MEAL

Steamed broccoli florets or broccolini (if you can find it) go extremely well when stirred right into the sauce in the last step. This will make for a more balanced meal when serving over pasta.

Orange Glazed Pork Chops

A Sunny Day Entrée (Whether It's Actually Sunny or Not)

These lip-smackingly good pork chops couldn't be any simpler to make. With just a few pork chops, one fresh orange, and a few pantry staples, you'll have dinner in no time.

SHOPPING LIST

1 tablespoon vegetable oil

4 thick-cut pork chops, about 1 ¼ inches thick

Salt and pepper

1 cup chicken stock or broth

1 teaspoon orange zest

¼ teaspoon dried thyme

¼ teaspoon onion powder

½ cup orange marmalade

2 tablespoons fresh orange juice

1 tablespoon apple cider vinegar

2 teaspoons soy sauce

1 teaspoon cornstarch

MAKE IT MEMORABLE

While prepping this, zest only ½ of an orange to collect the zest used in the recipe. If you juice that same half of the orange for the fresh orange juice used in the glaze you can thinly slice the other half of the orange to use as garnish.

1 WITH the cooker's lid off, heat oil on HIGH or "brown," until sizzling.

2 GENEROUSLY season the chops with salt and pepper, place in the cooker, and brown on each side.

3 ADD the chicken stock, orange zest, thyme, and onion powder to the cooker and securely lock the cooker's lid. Set for 15 minutes on HIGH.

4 LET the cooker's pressure release naturally 10 minutes before quick releasing any remaining pressure. Remove chops and let rest under aluminum foil.

5 DRAIN and discard all cooking liquid.

6 SET the cooker to HIGH or "brown" with lid off and whisk all remaining ingredients into it to create the glaze. Let cook just until combined and simmering. Toss pork chops in the glaze before serving.

PORK

Chinese Spareribs

Just as Addictive as Take-Out

These finger-licking ribs are a different take on the usual BBQ, but still lend the sweet and savory flavors from the sauce to keep you gnawing for quite a while.

PORK

SHOPPING LIST

1 teaspoon five-spice powder

¼ teaspoon salt

¼ teaspoon pepper

1 rack pork spareribs, cut to fit into cooker

2 cups chicken stock or broth

¼ cup hoisin sauce

¼ cup ketchup

2 tablespoons chili sauce

2 tablespoons light brown sugar

2 tablespoons soy sauce

1 tablespoon minced garlic

MAKE IT BETTER

Instead of baking, these are even better when grilled on a preheated grill for 10–15 minutes.

1 COMBINE together the five-spice powder, salt, and pepper, and then rub into the entire surface of the spareribs.

2 PLACE seasoned spareribs inside pressure cooker and add the chicken stock. Securely lock the cooker's lid and set for 12 minutes on HIGH.

3 LET the cooker's pressure release naturally for 15 minutes before performing a quick release to release any remaining pressure.

4 PREHEAT oven to 400°. Place the cooked ribs on a baking sheet that has been lined with aluminum foil.

5 IN a small mixing bowl, combine together the hoisin sauce, ketchup, chili sauce, brown sugar, soy sauce, and garlic.

6 SPREAD the sauce mixture onto the ribs, bake for 20 minutes, and then serve.

Pork Chops

with Creamy Mustard and Sage Gravy

The creamy mustard and sage gravy made in this recipe is amazingly addictive, especially when served with thick-cut pork chops. For best results, be sure to use whole grain or "course" mustard with visible seeds.

SHOPPING LIST

1 tablespoon vegetable oil

4 thick-cut pork chops, about 1 ¼ inches thick

Salt and pepper

1 cup chicken stock or broth

2 teaspoons chopped fresh sage

1 teaspoon light brown sugar

¼ teaspoon garlic powder

¼ cup whole-grain mustard

1 teaspoon cornstarch, mixed into 1 tablespoon water

3 tablespoons butter or margarine

CUT THE FAT

To make this into a lighter entrée, use lean center-cut pork loin chops and reduce the butter to only 1 tablespoon in the last step. Using margarine like Smart Balance will cut the fat even further.

1 WITH the cooker's lid off, heat oil on HIGH or "brown," until sizzling.

2 GENEROUSLY season the chops with salt and pepper, place in the cooker, and brown on each side.

3 ADD the chicken stock, sage, brown sugar, and garlic powder to the cooker and securely lock the cooker's lid. Set for 15 minutes on HIGH.

4 LET the cooker's pressure release naturally 10 minutes before quick releasing any remaining pressure. Remove chops and let rest under aluminum foil.

5 DRAIN off half of the cooking liquid and discard.

6 SET the cooker to HIGH or "brown" with lid off, and whisk the mustard and cornstarch into the remaining cooking liquid to create the gravy. Let simmer 2 minutes to thicken before turning cooker off and stirring in butter. Serve pork chops smothered in the gravy.

PORK

Prep Time	Cook Time	Temperature	Serves
10 min	70 min	High	8

Holy Mole Pork

Pork with a Secret Dash of Cocoa Powder

Mole (pronounced "mol-eh"), a Mexican chili sauce with a hint of chocolate, is becoming more and more popular throughout the United States. In this recipe, the chili is kept rather mild.

SHOPPING LIST

1 (4- to 5-pound) pork shoulder or butt

1 tablespoon chili powder

2 teaspoons salt

1 teaspoon pepper

1 cup beef stock or broth

¾ cup chili sauce

1 ½ teaspoons unsweetened cocoa powder

2 teaspoons ground cumin

½ teaspoon garlic powder

½ teaspoon onion powder

¼ teaspoon ground cinnamon

¼ cup raisins

1 tablespoon cornstarch, mixed into 1 tablespoon water

MAKE IT A MEAL

For a full meal, serve over yellow rice with a side of corn on the cob. Or try using this pork as an amazing burrito filling.

1 CUT pork into 2-inch thick slices (to speed up the cooking process).

2 COMBINE chili powder, salt, and pepper to create a dry rub. Rub onto the surface of all cuts of pork.

3 ADD beef stock, chili sauce, cocoa powder, cumin, garlic powder, onion powder, and cinnamon to the cooker. Securely lock the pressure cooker's lid and set for 70 minutes on HIGH.

4 LET the cooker's pressure release naturally for 10 minutes before quick releasing any remaining pressure.

5 WITH the cooker's lid off, set to HIGH or "brown." Add raisins and cornstarch mixture and let simmer, stirring occasionally, until sauce is thickened.

6 SERVE pork pulled and drizzled with the mole sauce.

PORK

Apple Cider Pork Roast

Tender and Moist Pork with Apple Flavor Throughout

This roast is cooked under pressure in an apple cider brine that leaves it with an irresistible flavor. Just be sure to drizzle the brine over the roast before serving to keep the meat nice and moist.

SHOPPING LIST

1 tablespoon vegetable oil

1 tablespoon butter or margarine

1 (3- to 4-pound) pork roast

Salt and pepper

3 cups apple cider

2 apples, cored and quartered

1 teaspoon salt

1 bay leaf

¼ teaspoon allspice

MAKE IT BETTER

Cooking the roast 80 minutes on HIGH will ensure that the roast is completely fork-tender and allow you to pull the meat and serve shredded rather than carved.

1 WITH the cooker's lid off, heat oil and butter on HIGH or "brown," until melted and sizzling.

2 GENEROUSLY season the roast with salt and pepper, place in the cooker, and brown on each side.

3 ADD the apple cider, apples, salt, bay leaf, and allspice to the cooker and securely lock the cooker's lid. Set for 65 minutes on HIGH.

4 LET the cooker's pressure release naturally 10 minutes before quick releasing any remaining pressure.

5 REMOVE roast, and let rest under aluminum foil 10 minutes before carving and serving drizzled with the cooking liquid.

Savory Sausage Bread Pudding

with Sage and Garlic

This savory take on bread pudding is a buttery, sausage-and-herb-filled casserole rather than the usually sweet treat.

SHOPPING LIST

Nonstick cooking spray

5–6 cups torn old or crusty bread

½ pound ground pork sausage, cooked and drained

5 large eggs

1 cup heavy cream

1 cup milk

2 tablespoons butter or margarine, melted

2 tablespoons chopped fresh sage

1 tablespoon minced garlic

1 tablespoon all-purpose flour

1 teaspoon salt

¼ teaspoon pepper

HELPFUL TIP

This can be prepped, wrapped, and refrigerated in the cake pans the night before for an even quicker breakfast or brunch.

PORK

1 SPRAY 2 (5-inch) metal cake pans or 1 (2-quart) soufflé dish with nonstick cooking spray.

2 TOSS together torn bread and sausage and add to the pans or dish, filling to the very top.

3 WHISK together remaining ingredients, and pour over top of the dry ingredients in the pans or dish, pressing the bread down to saturate. Let sit 10 minutes.

4 PLACE a small metal rack or trivet at the bottom of your pressure cooker. Pour 2 cups of water into the bottom of the cooker to create a water bath.

5 COVER pans or dish with aluminum foil, and place on metal rack in cooker (stacking the 2 cake pans).

6 SECURELY lock the cooker's lid and set for 25 minutes on HIGH.

7 LET the pressure release naturally for 10 minutes before performing a quick release for any remaining pressure. Let rest 15 minutes before serving.

Homemade Sausage Gravy

to Serve Over Warm Biscuits

No one will doubt how much you care about them when serving this rustic, traditional gravy. Just don't tell them it took five minutes to cook.

SHOPPING LIST

2 strips bacon, finely diced

1 pound ground pork sausage

1 tablespoon chopped fresh sage

½ cup chicken stock or broth

¼ cup all-purpose flour

1 ½ cups milk

1 teaspoon cracked black pepper

Salt to taste

Prepared biscuits

HELPFUL TIP

There are two tricks to making this perfect. The first is that you must use country-style pork sausage that is sold in a tube, not Italian pork sausage. The second is that you should use a very coarsely ground black pepper.

1 WITH the cooker's lid off, set to HIGH or "brown." Place bacon and sausage in the cooker, and sauté until browned, about 7 minutes.

2 ADD sage and chicken stock over top of the cooked meat in the cooker. Securely lock the pressure cooker's lid and set for 5 minutes on HIGH.

3 PERFORM a quick release to release the cooker's pressure.

4 IN a mixing bowl, whisk together flour and milk.

5 WITH the cooker's lid off, set to HIGH or "brown." Add the flour mixture to the cooker and simmer 3 minutes, or until thickened.

6 ADD cracked pepper and salt to the gravy, and then spoon over prepared biscuits to serve.

PORK

Kiss the Cook Baby Back Ribs

Kissed on the Grill for That Perfect Char

Baby Back Ribs are notorious for the time-consuming process it takes to get that perfect fall-off-the-bone texture. Here, with much less effort, I've taken one of my favorite American traditions and simplified it tremendously, sacrificing none of the succulence.

SHOPPING LIST

1 tablespoon paprika

1 tablespoon light brown sugar

½ teaspoon garlic powder

½ teaspoon onion powder

1 ½ teaspoons salt

¾ teaspoon pepper

1–2 racks baby back ribs, cut to fit into cooker

1 ½ cups chicken stock or broth

2 tablespoons ketchup

1 (18-ounce) bottle barbecue sauce

1 IN a small bowl or ramekin, combine paprika, brown sugar, garlic powder, onion powder, salt, and pepper. Rub the mixture evenly over entire surface of ribs.

2 PLACE rubbed ribs, chicken stock, and ketchup in the pressure cooker. Securely lock the cooker's lid and set for 15 minutes on HIGH.

3 LET the pressure cooker's pressure release naturally for 15 minutes before performing a quick release to release any remaining pressure.

4 GRILL cooked ribs using a preheated grill for 15 minutes, flipping once, and basting with barbecue sauce twice.

HELPFUL TIP

You can also prepare these in the oven after step 3. Simply preheat oven to 375°. Bake on an aluminum-lined sheet pan for 20–25 minutes.

PORK

Apricot Glazed Pork

Who Needs Applesauce?

Anyone who has ever had pork with applesauce knows that sweet and slightly acidic fruit make a perfect pair for nearly any cut of the meat. Apricots, like those in the glaze in this recipe, are no exception to this rule!

SHOPPING LIST

1 tablespoon vegetable oil

1 tablespoon butter or margarine

1 (2- to 3 ½-pound) pork loin roast

Salt and pepper

6 apricots, halved and pitted

1 cup chicken stock or broth

1 teaspoon dried thyme

½ cup apricot preserves

1 tablespoon Dijon mustard

1 teaspoon cornstarch, mixed into 1 tablespoon water

CUT THE COST

This can be made with any type of pork roast so be on the lookout for which cuts of meat are on sale. However, thicker roasts will take longer to cook. If your roast is not fork-tender when opening the cooker in step 4, simply close the lid and continue cooking under pressure 10–20 minutes.

1 WITH the cooker's lid off, heat oil and butter on HIGH or "brown," until melted and sizzling.

2 GENEROUSLY season the roast with salt and pepper, place in the cooker, and brown on each side.

3 ADD the apricots, chicken stock, and thyme to cooker, and securely lock the cooker's lid. Set for 45 minutes on HIGH.

4 LET the cooker's pressure release naturally 10 minutes before quick releasing any remaining pressure. Remove roast, and let rest under aluminum foil.

5 SET the cooker to HIGH or "brown" with lid off, and whisk the apricot preserves, Dijon mustard, and cornstarch and water mixture into the cooking liquid to create a glaze. Let simmer 2 minutes to thicken before returning roast to the glaze. Roll the roast in the glaze before carving and serving with additional glaze over top.

PORK

SEAFOOD

Shrimp Alfredo

Shrimp and Bow-Tie Pasta in a Creamy Sauce

Alfredo has been a longtime Italian favorite of mine, especially with shrimp. Here, I've chosen to use bow-tie pasta (farfalle) instead of the traditional fettuccine, as fettuccine would stick together in the cooker.

SHOPPING LIST

1 tablespoon olive oil

⅔ cup diced red onion

8 ounces farfalle pasta

12 ounces frozen shrimp

2 ½ cups chicken stock or broth

1 tablespoon minced garlic

1 teaspoon Old Bay Seasoning

½ cup heavy cream

1 cup grated Parmesan cheese

1 teaspoon all-purpose flour

Salt and pepper

Chopped parsley

1 WITH the cooker's lid off, heat oil and onion on HIGH or "brown," and sauté until onion is translucent, about 3 minutes.

2 ADD pasta, shrimp, chicken stock, garlic, and Old Bay Seasoning to the onion in the cooker.

3 SECURELY lock the pressure cooker's lid and set for 7 minutes on HIGH.

4 PERFORM a quick release to release the cooker's pressure.

5 SET the cooker to HIGH or "brown," and stir in heavy cream, Parmesan cheese, flour, and salt and pepper to taste. Let simmer 2 minutes. Sprinkle the chopped parsley over top before serving.

CUT THE FAT

Low-fat milk and 1 teaspoon additional flour can be used in place of the heavy cream to cut fat.

SEAFOOD

Tender Poached Salmon

with Lemon and Tarragon

This recipe for poached salmon is rich with bright flavors and couldn't get much easier. With very little preparation, all you have to do is throw it in the pot.

SHOPPING LIST

3 tablespoons butter or margarine

1 ½–2 pounds salmon fillets

1 cup chicken stock or broth

1 tablespoon minced garlic

Juice of 1 lemon

1 tablespoon chopped fresh parsley

1 tablespoon chopped fresh tarragon

1 tablespoon light brown sugar

¼ teaspoon salt

⅛ teaspoon pepper

1 ADD all ingredients to the cooker.

2 SECURELY lock the pressure cooker's lid and set for 6 minutes on HIGH.

3 PERFORM a quick release to release the cooker's pressure.

4 SERVE immediately, drizzled in juices from the cooker.

MAKE IT BETTER

You can make this even better by adding 2 tablespoons of a dry white wine in step 1.

SEAFOOD

Scallops Veracruzano

with Tomatoes, Green Olives, and Jalapeño

The brine from the olives and the spice from the pepper certainly jump out at you, but they also truly complement the very tender sea scallops in this amazingly light recipe.

SHOPPING LIST

1 tablespoon olive oil

1 red onion, thinly sliced

1 jalapeño pepper, seeded and chopped

2 tomatoes, diced

1 tablespoon minced garlic

1 tablespoon chopped fresh oregano

½ cup roughly chopped green olives

⅓ cup chicken stock or broth

1 ½ pounds sea scallops, rinsed

Juice of ½ lime

Salt and pepper

1 WITH the cooker's lid off, heat oil on HIGH or "brown," until sizzling.

2 PLACE onion and jalapeño pepper in the cooker, and sauté, just until onion is translucent.

3 ADD tomatoes, garlic, oregano, olives, and chicken stock to the cooker, and stir.

4 PLACE scallops on top of everything in the cooker. Squeeze lime juice over top, and sprinkle with salt and pepper.

5 SECURELY lock the pressure cooker's lid and set for 2 minutes on HIGH.

6 PERFORM a quick release to release the cooker's pressure. Serve immediately.

MAKE IT BETTER

When it comes to this recipe, the more spice the better. If you like it hot, add ½ teaspoon of crushed red pepper flakes in step 3.

SEAFOOD

Lemon and Dill Fish Packets

Flaky White Fish, All Wrapped Up

With the light flavors of lemon, butter, and dill combined with your favorite white fish all wrapped up in packets and under pressure for just five minutes, it'll be like giving yourself a present.

SHOPPING LIST

2 tilapia or cod fillets

Salt, pepper, and garlic powder

2 sprigs fresh dill

4 slices lemon

2 tablespoons butter

MAKE IT MEMORABLE

There is no need to remove the fish from the packets before serving. In fact, it makes a really nice presentation.

1   LAY out 2 large squares of parchment paper.

2   PLACE a fillet in the center of each parchment square, and then season with a generous amount of salt, pepper, and garlic powder.

3   ON each fillet, place in order: 1 sprig of dill, 2 lemon slices, and 1 tablespoon of butter.

4   FOR best results, place a small metal rack or trivet at the bottom of your pressure cooker. Pour 1 cup of water into the cooker to create a water bath.

5   CLOSE up parchment paper around the fillets, folding to seal, and then place both packets on metal rack inside cooker.

6   SECURELY lock the pressure cooker's lid and set for 5 minutes on HIGH.

7   PERFORM a quick release to release the cooker's pressure. Unwrap packets and serve.

SEAFOOD

Manhattan Clam Chowder

You Know, the Red One

In some parts of the North and usually on Fridays, it's quite customary to go out to your favorite restaurant and enjoy a bowl of this hearty, tomato-based chowder. With this recipe, you can have it whenever you like. Just don't forget to add the clams in the last step!

SHOPPING LIST

2 (6 ½-ounce) cans baby clams, liquid reserved

4 strips thick-cut bacon, diced

1 yellow onion, diced

1 small green bell pepper, diced

3 stalks celery, diced

2 cups cubed potatoes (½-inch cubes)

1 (14 ½-ounce) can diced tomatoes

1 ½ cups tomato juice

2 tablespoons tomato paste

2 bay leaves

1 teaspoon dry oregano

½ teaspoon dry thyme

Salt and pepper

1 DRAIN the clams, reserving the juice, and then set aside.

2 WITH the pressure cooker's lid off, set to HIGH or "brown," combine bacon and onion in the cooker, and sauté until bacon is crispy and onions are lightly caramelized.

3 ADD reserved clam broth and remaining ingredients, except for the clams. Securely lock the pressure cooker's lid and set for 6 minutes on HIGH.

4 PERFORM a quick release to release the cooker's pressure, and then set the cooker to HIGH or "brown."

5 ADD clams to the cooker and let simmer, stirring occasionally, until clams are warm and potatoes are fork-tender. Remove bay leaves, add salt and pepper to taste, and serve immediately.

MAKE IT BETTER

Though this is very different from New England Clam Chowder, you can make a creamy red broth by stirring in ½ cup of heavy cream in the last step.

SEAFOOD

Bouillabaisse

Shrimp, Mussels, and Cod in a Tomato-Based Broth

This variation of the French seafood soup is both delicate and complex in flavor, an instance in which a little prep work goes a long way.

SHOPPING LIST

2 tablespoons olive oil

1 red onion, diced

1 (14-ounce) can diced tomatoes, with juice

1 (8-ounce) can tomato sauce

2 cups chicken stock or broth

1 cup clam juice

½ pound large shrimp

8 mussels, scrubbed

½ pound cod, thickly sliced

1 tablespoon minced garlic

1 teaspoon dried thyme

1 teaspoon sugar

1 tiny pinch saffron threads, crushed

1 bay leaf

Salt and pepper

1 WITH the cooker's lid off, heat oil on HIGH or "brown," until sizzling. Place onion in cooker, and sauté until translucent, 4–5 minutes.

2 ADD tomatoes, tomato sauce, chicken stock, clam juice, shrimp, mussels, cod, garlic, thyme, sugar, saffron, and bay leaf.

3 SECURELY lock the pressure cooker's lid and set for 5 minutes on HIGH.

4 LET the cooker's pressure release naturally for 5 minutes before quick releasing any remaining pressure. Add salt and pepper to taste before serving.

SEAFOOD

MAKE IT A MEAL

Serve into a bowl of white or yellow rice for an even heartier meal.

Tender Tuna Steaks

with White Wine, Butter, and Capers

This amazingly light dish keeps things simple and delicious, with a buttery, sweet sauce speckled in capers, adding a briny, peppery bite.

SHOPPING LIST

2 pounds tuna steaks, 1 inch thick

¼ cup white wine

¼ cup chicken stock or broth

1 tablespoon minced garlic

1 sprig fresh thyme

6 tablespoons butter

2 tablespoons capers

Salt and pepper

1 ADD tuna steaks, white wine, chicken stock, garlic, and thyme to the cooker.

2 SECURELY lock the pressure cooker's lid and set for 4 minutes on HIGH.

3 LET the cooker's pressure release naturally for 5 minutes before quick releasing any remaining pressure.

4 DRAIN ½ of the cooking liquid, and stir in butter and capers. Add salt and pepper to taste before serving.

MAKE IT YOURS

Though the alcohol cooks out, the wine in this recipe can be replaced with the juice of 1 lemon, if desired.

SEAFOOD

Caribbean Salmon

with Fresh Mango

This island inspired dish adds the flavors of freshly squeezed lime juice and sliced mango at the very end, keeping things bright and different from the usual fare.

SHOPPING LIST

1 cup chicken stock or broth

1 ½–2 pounds salmon fillets

¼ cup finely diced red onion

1 tablespoon olive oil

1 teaspoon ground allspice

1 teaspoon light brown sugar

½ teaspoon ground cumin

½ teaspoon dried thyme

¼ teaspoon salt

¼ teaspoon pepper

1 lime, halved

1 mango, peeled and thinly sliced

MAKE IT A MEAL

For a full Caribbean meal, serve over yellow rice with a side of fried plantains. You can even buy frozen precooked plantains in most grocery stores these days.

1 FOR best results, place a metal rack or trivet at the bottom of the pressure cooker.

2 POUR in chicken stock, and then place salmon fillets on the metal rack in cooker.

3 IN a small mixing bowl, combine the onion, oil, allspice, brown sugar, cumin, thyme, salt, and pepper. Spread the onion mixture over top of salmon on rack.

4 SECURELY lock the pressure cooker's lid and set for 6 minutes on HIGH.

5 PERFORM a quick release to release the cooker's pressure.

6 SQUEEZE the lime halves over the cooked salmon, and then top with mango slices before serving.

SEAFOOD

Cajun Crab Risotto

A Gourmet Meal in Only Minutes

This risotto is filled with jumbo lump crabmeat for a truly luxurious meal. I make this even creamier than ordinary risottos by stirring in just a little bit of cream cheese, which pairs so well with the crab.

SHOPPING LIST

1 tablespoon olive oil

1 tablespoon butter or margarine

1 small yellow onion, diced

2 cups Arborio or Calrose rice

5 cups chicken broth or stock

¼ cup dry white wine, may use additional chicken stock

1 teaspoon Old Bay Seasoning

¼ cup grated Parmesan cheese

2 ounces cream cheese

6–8 ounces jumbo lump crabmeat

Salt and pepper

Chopped fresh chives, for garnish

1 WITH the cooker's lid off, heat oil and butter on HIGH or "brown," until melted and sizzling.

2 PLACE the onion in the cooker, and sauté until translucent, about 5 minutes.

3 STIR in rice, and sauté 1 additional minute.

4 ADD the chicken broth, white wine, and Old Bay Seasoning. Securely lock the pressure cooker's lid and set for 6 minutes on HIGH.

5 PERFORM a quick release to release the cooker's pressure. Stir in Parmesan and cream cheeses before gently folding in crabmeat. Season with salt and pepper to taste before serving sprinkled with chopped chives.

CUT THE COST

I will admit that jumbo lump crabmeat, which is usually sold in small refrigerated containers in the seafood department, can be quite expensive. While it isn't the same, you can save a lot of money on this recipe by substituting 1 cup of finely chopped imitation crabmeat in its place.

SEAFOOD

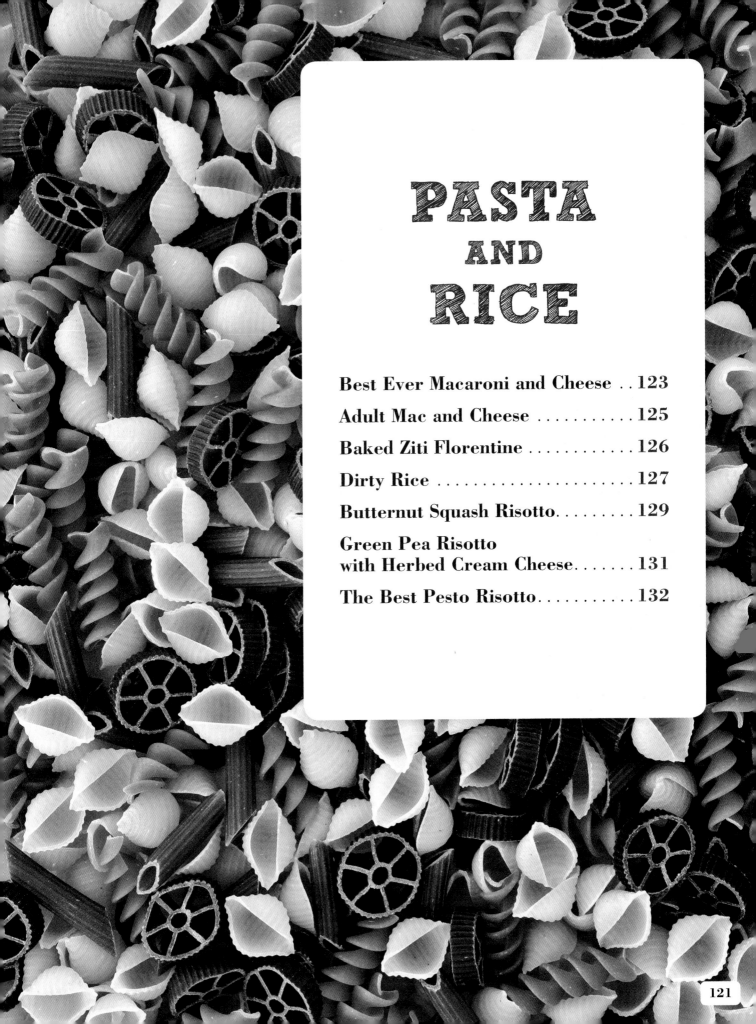

PASTA AND RICE

Best Ever Macaroni and Cheese

My Most Popular Recipe, Made Even Better

When I first wrote a recipe for macaroni and cheese made in a pressure cooker, I had no idea it would become my most requested recipe of all time. While the comments were overwhelmingly positive, I took some of the legitimate criticisms and set out to improve upon my original recipe...creating a thicker and creamier sauce that sets even quicker than the original.

SHOPPING LIST

3 cups elbow macaroni

2 cups chicken stock or broth

1 cup water

2 tablespoons butter or margarine

2 tablespoons grated
Parmesan cheese

¼ teaspoon salt

⅛ teaspoon white pepper

2 cups shredded sharp
Cheddar cheese

4 ounces processed cheese
(like Velveeta)

1 ADD elbow macaroni, chicken stock, water, butter, Parmesan cheese, salt, and white pepper to the pressure cooker.

2 SECURELY lock the pressure cooker's lid and set for 6 minutes on HIGH.

3 PERFORM a quick release to release the cooker's pressure.

4 STIR in shredded Cheddar cheese and processed cheese until both cheeses are melted and creamy. Let sit 5 minutes to thicken before serving.

MAKE IT MY WAY

I like to add just a teaspoon of yellow or Dijon mustard in my macaroni and cheese in the last step. This was a love it or hate it thing amongst those who prepared my old recipe, so I have decided to leave it out here (opting for the lesser tang of white pepper instead). If you are feeling adventurous though, I highly suggest giving the mustard a try!

Adult Mac and Cheese

Because We Are All Kids at Heart

This more refined take on macaroni and cheese swaps elbow macaroni for mini penne pasta and adds bacon, onion, and red bell pepper to a white Cheddar and Gorgonzola cream sauce that all palates, sophisticated or otherwise, can enjoy!

SHOPPING LIST

4 strips bacon

⅔ cup diced red onion

3 cups mini penne pasta

3 ¼ cups chicken stock or broth

¼ teaspoon garlic powder

¼ teaspoon salt

¼ teaspoon pepper

1 ¼ cups shredded white Cheddar cheese

¼ cup crumbled Gorgonzola cheese

4 ounces cream cheese

¼ cup finely diced red bell pepper

MAKE IT MEMORABLE

Truffle salt is one of the most amazing (and adult) things you can top macaroni and cheese with. It adds an amazing and earthy flavor that you simply can't get any other way. While it can be expensive and hard to find in stores, you can find it online for as little as $12 for a jar that will last a very, very long time.

1 WITH the cooker's lid off, heat bacon on HIGH or "brown," until bacon is crisp. Remove bacon, crumble, and reserve.

2 ADD onion to the bacon grease in the cooker, and cook 2–3 minutes, just until translucent.

3 ADD penne pasta, chicken stock, garlic powder, salt, and pepper to the pressure cooker.

4 SECURELY lock the pressure cooker's lid and set for 6 minutes on HIGH.

5 PERFORM a quick release to release the cooker's pressure.

6 ADD reserved bacon crumbles and remaining ingredients to the cooker, stirring until cheese is melted and creamy. Let sit 5 minutes to thicken before serving.

PASTA

Baked Ziti Florentine

Pasta with Tomato Sauce, Spinach, and a Thick Layer of Three Cheeses

This meatless version of an Italian favorite shares the same rustic appeal as lasagna, only with less preparation time before putting under pressure.

SHOPPING LIST

2 tablespoons olive oil

1 yellow onion, diced

1 (24-ounce) jar chunky spaghetti sauce

2 ½ cups vegetable stock or broth

4 cups fresh spinach leaves

5 leaves fresh basil, chopped

2 ½ cups ziti pasta

1 pound whole milk ricotta cheese

1 large egg

¼ cup grated Parmesan cheese

¼ teaspoon garlic powder

½ teaspoon Italian seasoning

¼ teaspoon salt

⅛ teaspoon pepper

1 ½ cups grated mozzarella cheese

1 WITH the cooker's lid off, heat oil on HIGH or "brown," until sizzling.

2 PLACE onions in the cooker, and cook until translucent, about 3 minutes.

3 ADD spaghetti sauce, vegetable broth, spinach, and basil to the cooker, and let simmer until spinach cooks down, about 2 minutes. Turn off heat and stir in pasta.

4 IN a large mixing bowl, use a fork to whisk together ricotta cheese, egg, Parmesan cheese, garlic powder, Italian seasoning, salt, and pepper.

5 COVER the pasta mixture in the pot with the ricotta mixture.

6 SECURELY lock the cooker's lid and set for 6 minutes on HIGH. Perform a quick release to release the cooker's pressure, remove cover, and sprinkle with the mozzarella cheese. Re-cover and let rest at least 5 minutes before serving.

CUT THE FAT

Part-skim ricotta cheese and two egg whites can be used in place of the whole milk ricotta and egg in this recipe to cut the fat, though the final result may not hold together as well.

PASTA

Dirty Rice

with Spicy Pork Sausage

While true Cajun Dirty Rice is made with chicken giblets and livers to get its brown color, I make mine with spicy pork sausage (to most people's relief). But just because I don't follow ALL the rules, doesn't mean this doesn't pack a ton of Cajun flavor!

SHOPPING LIST

2 tablespoons olive oil

8 ounces spicy ground pork sausage

1 small yellow onion, diced

1 small green bell pepper, diced

3 stalks celery, diced

1 tablespoon minced garlic

2 cups long-grain white rice (uncooked)

1 teaspoon dry oregano

1 teaspoon chili powder

1 teaspoon paprika

¼ teaspoon pepper

2 ¼ cups chicken stock or broth

1 WITH the cooker's lid off, heat oil on HIGH or "brown," until sizzling.

2 PLACE the sausage, onion, bell pepper, and celery in the cooker, and sauté until sausage has browned, about 5–7 minutes.

3 STIR in garlic, rice, oregano, chili powder, paprika, and pepper, and sauté 1 additional minute.

4 ADD the chicken stock and securely lock the pressure cooker's lid. Set for 4 minutes on HIGH.

5 LET the pressure release naturally for 10 minutes before performing a quick release to release any remaining pressure. Depending on the salt content of the sausage and chicken stock, you may need to salt to taste before serving.

CUT THE FAT

As this is great with pretty much any kind of sausage, ground turkey sausage can be used to cut the fat. You can even use sliced low-fat kielbasa or chicken sausages.

PASTA

Butternut Squash Risotto

Yes, It Tastes as Good as It Looks

This creamy risotto is like a (most wonderful) marriage of risotto and a puréed butternut squash soup—an absolutely perfect dish for fall.

SHOPPING LIST

2 cups cubed butternut squash

1 cup water

1 tablespoon olive oil

1 tablespoon butter or margarine

1 small yellow onion, diced

2 cups Arborio or Calrose rice

5 cups chicken broth or stock

1 tablespoon cider vinegar

1 tablespoon chopped fresh sage

½ teaspoon ground cinnamon

⅓ cup half-and-half

1 ½ tablespoons light brown sugar

Salt to taste

MAKE IT EASIER

Many grocery stores now carry bags of cubed butternut squash in the frozen vegetable case. (Some even have frozen mashed squash!) These can usually be microwaved according to the bag's directions, saving you from having to cut and dice the squash yourself.

1 PLACE cubed squash and water in pressure cooker, securely lock the cooker's lid, and set for 6 minutes on HIGH.

2 PERFORM a quick release to release the cooker's pressure. Drain the cooked squash and transfer to a large mixing bowl. Use a potato masher, heavy fork, or food processor to mash the squash well.

3 MEANWHILE, with the cooker's lid off, heat oil and butter on HIGH or "brown," until melted and sizzling.

4 PLACE the onion in the cooker, and sauté until translucent, about 5 minutes.

5 STIR in rice, and sauté 1 additional minute.

6 ADD the mashed squash and remaining ingredients, except half-and-half. Securely lock the pressure cooker's lid and set for 6 minutes on HIGH.

7 PERFORM a quick release to release the cooker's pressure. Stir in half-and-half, and add salt to taste before serving.

PASTA

Green Pea Risotto

with Herbed Cream Cheese

The sweet peas in this risotto are perfectly offset by savory herbed cream cheese that you serve dolloped over top (so you can watch and salivate as it melts into the creamy rice).

SHOPPING LIST

1 tablespoon olive oil

1 tablespoon butter or margarine

1 small yellow onion, diced

2 cups Arborio or Calrose rice

5 cups vegetable broth or stock

¼ cup dry white wine, may use additional vegetable stock

2 teaspoons minced garlic

1 bay leaf

2 cups frozen peas, thawed

Salt and pepper

5–8 ounces herbed cream cheese spread

HELPFUL TIP

There are many different brands and flavors of herbed cheese or cream cheese spreads that will work well atop this risotto. Boursin and Rondele brands are usually sold in the specialty cheese case, but you should also be able to find flavored Philadelphia brand cream cheese in the regular cheese section.

1   WITH the cooker's lid off, heat oil and butter on HIGH or "brown," until melted and sizzling.

2   PLACE the onion in the cooker, and sauté until translucent, about 5 minutes.

3   STIR in rice, and sauté 1 additional minute.

4   ADD the vegetable broth, white wine, garlic, and bay leaf. Securely lock the pressure cooker's lid and set for 6 minutes on HIGH.

5   MEANWHILE, place 1 cup of the thawed peas in a food processor, and pulse until fully puréed.

6   PERFORM a quick release to release the cooker's pressure. Stir both the puréed and whole peas into the risotto, and then season with salt and pepper to taste.

7   SERVE each bowl of risotto topped with a large dollop of the herbed cream cheese.

PASTA

The Best Pesto Risotto

with Mascarpone Cheese

If you've ever read any of my previous cookbooks, you'll know that I'm a pretty big fan of fresh basil pesto. One of my favorite ways to use that fresh pesto is in this exact risotto recipe.

SHOPPING LIST

1 tablespoon vegetable oil

1 tablespoon butter or margarine

1 small yellow onion, diced

2 cups Arborio or Calrose rice

5 cups chicken broth or stock

2 tablespoons lemon juice

1 teaspoon sugar

1 ½ cups fresh basil leaves

½ cup grated Parmesan cheese

⅓ cup extra virgin olive oil

¼ cup pine nuts

3 cloves garlic

Salt and pepper

4 ounces mascarpone cheese

CUT THE COST

Purchasing an 8-ounce jar or tub of prepared pesto sauce can save you money over buying the ingredients fresh, but the quality can sometimes lack. Cream cheese can be used in place of the mascarpone cheese to cut the cost even further or if your store doesn't stock mascarpone.

1 WITH the cooker's lid off, heat vegetable oil and butter on HIGH or "brown," until melted and sizzling.

2 PLACE the onion in the cooker, and sauté until translucent, about 5 minutes.

3 STIR in rice, and sauté 1 additional minute.

4 ADD the chicken broth, lemon juice, and sugar. Securely lock the pressure cooker's lid and set for 6 minutes on HIGH.

5 MEANWHILE, create the pesto by placing basil, Parmesan cheese, olive oil, pine nuts, and garlic in a food processor and pulsing until almost entirely smooth.

6 PERFORM a quick release to release the cooker's pressure. Stir the pesto into the risotto, and then season with salt and pepper to taste.

7 SERVE each bowl of risotto topped with a large dollop of mascarpone cheese.

VEGETABLES AND SIDES

The Best Brussels Sprouts

with Bacon and Onions

This is another one of those instances where bacon just makes things better, even Brussels sprouts, which are truly one-of-a-kind on their own.

SHOPPING LIST

1 teaspoon vegetable oil

4 strips thick bacon, diced

1 yellow onion, thinly sliced

1 pound Brussels sprouts, ends trimmed and halved

½ cup chicken stock or broth

1 tablespoon minced garlic

1 teaspoon lemon juice

2 teaspoons light brown sugar

¼ teaspoon onion powder

¼ teaspoon salt

¼ teaspoon pepper

1 WITH the cooker's lid off, heat oil on HIGH or "brown," until sizzling.

2 ADD bacon and onion to the cooker, and sauté until bacon is crisp and onion begins to caramelize.

3 ADD remaining ingredients to the cooker.

4 SECURELY lock the pressure cooker's lid and set for 2 minutes on HIGH.

5 PERFORM a quick release to release the cooker's pressure. Serve immediately.

HELPFUL TIP

To save time, you can prepare this recipe without halving the Brussels sprouts by simply cooking for 4 minutes instead of 2.

SIDES

Broccoli and Cheese Mashed Potatoes

One Way to Get Kids to Eat Their Vegetables

Cheese certainly has the power to make things even better. With this fantastically green side dish, I've taken two things cheese pairs well with—broccoli and potatoes—and combined all that greatness together.

SHOPPING LIST

6 russet potatoes, peeled and quartered

1 ½ cups frozen broccoli florets

2 cups water

3 tablespoons butter

¼ cup half-and-half

⅔ cup shredded sharp Cheddar cheese

¼ teaspoon onion powder

½ teaspoon salt

¼ teaspoon pepper

1 ADD potatoes, broccoli florets, and water to the pot. Securely lock the pressure cooker's lid and set for 6 minutes on HIGH.

2 PERFORM a quick release to release the cooker's pressure.

3 DRAIN the cooked potatoes and broccoli and then return all to the cooker. Using a heavy fork or potato masher, mash both potatoes and broccoli, until mostly smooth, adding remaining ingredients as you go. Serve immediately.

HELPFUL TIP

Be sure to buy "premium" or "select" frozen broccoli florets for this recipe, otherwise you will be stuck with a lot of stems that don't easily mash into the potatoes.

SIDES

Squash Casserole

with a Creamy, Cheesy Sauce and Chopped Pecans

Yellow squash can be a nice change of pace when it comes to vegetables. There simply isn't anything quite like the earthy sweetness in this recipe, combined with creamy cheese melted right in and topped with nutty pecan pieces.

SHOPPING LIST

1 tablespoon vegetable oil

1 yellow onion, diced

6 cups thick-cubed yellow squash

⅓ cup chicken stock or broth

2 tablespoons butter or margarine, melted

¼ teaspoon dried thyme

½ teaspoon salt

¼ teaspoon pepper

⅛ teaspoon ground nutmeg

4 ounces cream cheese, cubed

1 cup shredded sharp Cheddar cheese

¼ cup chopped pecans

1 WITH the cooker's lid off, heat oil on HIGH or "brown," until sizzling. Place onion in cooker and sauté until translucent, 4–5 minutes.

2 ADD yellow squash, chicken stock, melted butter, thyme, salt, pepper, and nutmeg. Securely lock the pressure cooker's lid and set for 2 minutes on HIGH.

3 PERFORM a quick release to release the cooker's pressure.

4 STIR in cream cheese and sharp Cheddar cheese until melted. Serve topped with chopped pecans.

HELPFUL TIP

Though it may seem unnecessary to cube the cream cheese, this helps it melt faster, keeping you from over-stirring the delicate squash.

SIDES

Cheesy Spoonbread

Like Cornbread That You Eat with a Spoon

This delicious southern side dish falls somewhere in the category of a savory pudding or soufflé. Regardless of what exactly it is, I hold it in almost as high of regard as I do cornbread.

SHOPPING LIST

Nonstick cooking spray

1 cup milk

2 cups chicken stock or broth

1 cup Bisquick baking mix

⅔ cup cornmeal

1 cup shredded sharp Cheddar cheese

1 large egg

2 tablespoons butter or margarine, melted

2 teaspoons sugar

1 teaspoon salt

½ teaspoon garlic powder

1 COAT the cooker's pot with an even amount of the nonstick cooking spray.

2 IN a mixing bowl, combine remaining ingredients, and then add to the cooker.

3 SECURELY lock the pressure cooker's lid and set for 8 minutes on LOW.

4 PERFORM a quick release to release the cooker's pressure. Spoonbread will still be quite runny. Stir well, using a potato masher to mash the cooked cornmeal at the bottom into the rest of the liquid.

5 COVER, but leave steam valve open and do not secure lid. Set to HIGH or "brown" and let cook for 5 minutes. Turn off heat and let rest at least 5 minutes before serving.

MAKE IT BETTER

Try adding 1 cup of thawed frozen corn kernels to the spoonbread batter in step 2 to liven things up.

SIDES

Collard Greens

A Southern Staple

While collard greens are a leafy green vegetable, many people are surprised to learn that they take up to an hour of simmering on the stove to cook down and get tender! My recipe (and a pressure cooker) cuts that time all the way down to 15 minutes!

SHOPPING LIST

4 strips thick-cut bacon, diced

½ cup diced yellow onion

2 bunches collard greens, rinsed very well and coarsely chopped

1 ¾ cups chicken stock or broth

2 teaspoons minced garlic

⅛ teaspoon salt

⅛ teaspoon pepper

1 With the cooker's lid off, heat bacon and onion on HIGH or "brown," until bacon is nearly crisp, about 5 minutes.

2 Add remaining ingredients and securely lock the pressure cooker's lid. Set for 15 minutes on HIGH.

3 Let the pressure release naturally for 5 minutes before performing a quick release for any remaining pressure. Serve using a slotted spoon.

MAKE IT BETTER

You can also make this with a ham hock in place of the bacon. Simply skip the first step, adding all ingredients at once. Just remember to pull the meat from the ham hock and stir into the greens before serving.

Creamy Succotash

with Fresh Corn, Sugar Snap Peas, and Bell Pepper

Although this succulent side is bursting with fresh and snappy vegetables, cream cheese is the real star, melting in right at the last minute.

SHOPPING LIST

1 tablespoon vegetable oil

1 yellow onion, diced

4 cups fresh corn kernels, cut off the cob

3 cups sugar snap peas

½ cup chicken stock or broth

1 teaspoon dried thyme

¼ teaspoon garlic powder

¾ teaspoon salt

¼ teaspoon pepper

½ cup finely diced red bell pepper

6 ounces cream cheese, cubed

1 WITH the cooker's lid off, heat oil and onion on HIGH or "brown," and sauté until onion is translucent, about 3 minutes.

2 ADD corn, snap peas, chicken stock, thyme, garlic powder, salt, and pepper. Securely lock the pressure cooker's lid and set for 3 minutes on HIGH.

3 PERFORM a quick release to release the cooker's pressure.

4 STIR in red bell pepper and cream cheese before serving.

MAKE IT BETTER

Try using herbed cream cheese or cheese spread in place of the regular cream cheese for even more flavor.

SIDES

Winter Vegetable Ratatouille

with Parsnips, Rutabagas, and Grape Tomatoes

Ratatouille is such a wonderful way to enjoy fresh, seasonal vegetables. With this version of the French stew, you'll be surprised by how the flavors mingle together in a fraction of the time it usually takes.

SHOPPING LIST

1 tablespoon vegetable oil

1 large red onion, thinly sliced

4 parsnips, cut into 1-inch lengths

3 cups peeled and cubed rutabagas

1 pint grape tomatoes

3 carrots, cut into 1-inch lengths

1 cup chicken stock or broth

2 cloves garlic, thinly sliced

2 tablespoons chopped fresh sage

2 tablespoons light brown sugar

¼ teaspoon ground cinnamon

1 teaspoon salt

¼ teaspoon pepper

3 tablespoons butter or margarine, melted

1 WITH the cooker's lid off, heat oil on HIGH or "brown," until sizzling.

2 PLACE onion in cooker and sauté until translucent, 4–5 minutes.

3 ADD parsnips, rutabagas, tomatoes, carrots, chicken stock, garlic, sage, brown sugar, cinnamon, salt, and pepper to the cooker.

4 POUR melted butter over top vegetables, securely lock the pressure cooker's lid, and set for 4 minutes on HIGH.

5 PERFORM a quick release to release the cooker's pressure. Serve immediately.

HELPFUL TIP

Be sure to cut and cube the vegetables at least 1 inch thick, as these roots cook quick under pressure!

SIDES

Italian Polenta

Like Grits...Only Italian!

This creamy sidekick goes great with any of your favorite proteins, warming your belly in the same fashion as its Southern American cousin.

SHOPPING LIST

2 tablespoons olive oil

¼ cup finely minced yellow onion

4 ½ cups chicken stock or broth

1 ½ cups coarse cornmeal (polenta)

¼ teaspoon garlic powder

¾ teaspoon salt

¼ teaspoon pepper

⅓ cup grated Parmesan cheese

3 tablespoons butter or margarine

1 WITH the cooker's lid off, heat oil on HIGH or "brown," until sizzling.

2 PLACE the onion in the cooker, and sauté 1 minute.

3 ADD the chicken broth, cornmeal, garlic powder, salt, and pepper. Securely lock the pressure cooker's lid and set for 9 minutes on HIGH.

4 PERFORM a quick release to release the cooker's pressure. Stir in Parmesan cheese and butter before serving.

MAKE IT A MEAL

Creamy polenta goes great with meaty entrées that have a robust sauce or gravy, as the sauce will pool into the polenta and lend it its flavors.

SIDES

Loaded Mashed Potatoes

with Sour Cream, Bacon, and Cheddar Cheese

Just about everyone can appreciate a hearty portion of cheesy, creamy mashed potatoes. They go with almost anything. And topping them with crispy bacon bits and fresh green onion slices elevates them to yet another level of deliciousness.

SHOPPING LIST

4 slices bacon

6 russet potatoes, peeled and quartered

2 cups water

3 tablespoons butter

½ cup sour cream

¼ cup grated Parmesan cheese

¼ teaspoon garlic powder

½ teaspoon salt

¼ teaspoon pepper

½ cup shredded Cheddar cheese

4 scallions, thinly sliced

HELPFUL TIP

It is best to mash the sour cream into the potatoes a little bit at a time, just to make sure that the potatoes don't get soupy.

1 WITH the cooker's lid off, heat bacon on HIGH or "brown," until crisp. Remove bacon, finely chop, and set aside. Drain all but 2 teaspoons of the bacon grease.

2 ADD potatoes and water to the pot, securely lock the pressure cooker's lid, and set for 6 minutes on HIGH.

3 PERFORM a quick release to release the cooker's pressure. Drain the cooked potatoes and return them to the pot.

4 USING a heavy fork or potato masher, mash potatoes until mostly smooth, adding the butter, sour cream, Parmesan cheese, garlic powder, salt, and pepper as you go along.

5 TOP with finely chopped bacon, Cheddar cheese, and scallions before serving warm.

SIDES

Boston Baked Beans

Baked from Scratch, Without Any Baking

This, my favorite recipe for Boston "Baked" Beans, is actually an amalgamation of the traditional version (with a heavy molasses flavor) and the more modern versions (with ketchup) that it has evolved into over the years.

SHOPPING LIST

2 cups small navy (white) beans (dry)

6 strips thick-cut bacon, diced

1 large yellow onion, diced

3 cups water

1 tablespoon olive oil

½ teaspoon dry mustard

⅛ teaspoon ground cloves

¼ teaspoon pepper

⅓ cup ketchup

⅓ cup molasses

⅓ cup light brown sugar

3 tablespoons yellow mustard

MAKE IT FASTER

You can make this without presoaking the beans for 30 minutes simply by adding 5 minutes to the cooking time in step 3.

1 SOAK navy beans for 30 minutes as you prep the remaining ingredients. Drain and rinse the soaked beans.

2 WITH the cooker's lid off, heat bacon and onion on HIGH or "brown," until bacon is nearly crisp, about 5 minutes.

3 ADD the soaked beans, water, olive oil, dry mustard, ground cloves, and pepper, and securely lock the pressure cooker's lid. Set for 20 minutes on HIGH.

4 LET the pressure release naturally for 10 minutes before performing a quick release for any remaining pressure.

5 SET the cooker to HIGH or "brown," and stir in remaining ingredients. Let simmer 5 minutes, adding water if the sauce is too thick to stir.

SIDES

LIGHTER FARE

Creamy Eggplant Dip

A Fresh and Hearty Alternative for Chips

Eggplants are surprisingly perfect for pressure cooking, especially when it comes to turning them into a delicious and naturally healthy spread or dip. And worry not—there is so much flavor here, it'll disappear before your very eyes.

SHOPPING LIST

2 globe eggplants, quartered

½ teaspoon Italian seasoning

1 cup water

2 tablespoons extra virgin olive oil

Juice of ½ lemon

1 tablespoon chopped fresh oregano

1 tablespoon minced garlic

¾ teaspoon salt

¼ teaspoon pepper

NUTRITION

Calories: 90

Fat: 5g

Total Carbs: 11.5g

Fiber: 6.5g

Protein: 2g

1 PLACE eggplants, Italian seasoning, and water in cooker. Securely lock the pressure cooker's lid and set for 8 minutes on HIGH.

2 PERFORM a quick release to release the cooker's pressure.

3 REMOVE cooked eggplant from the pressure cooker and scoop away from skin.

4 PLACE eggplant meat and remaining ingredients in a food processor, and pulse until the mixture is smooth.

5 SERVE warm or chilled, alongside whole-wheat pita chips or fresh, crispy vegetables (such as cucumber, broccoli, carrots, and celery sticks).

LIGHTER

Traditional Minestrone Soup

Full-Flavored, No Sacrifices

One of the most common dishes you might find on an Italian menu is in fact minestrone soup, almost as popular as any pasta dish. It is naturally pretty light, so no sacrifices had to be made to fit it into this section.

SHOPPING LIST

2 tablespoons olive oil

1 yellow onion, diced

3 carrots, coarsely chopped

2 stalks celery, coarsely chopped

2 zucchini, cut into thick half-moons

3 cups fresh spinach leaves

4 cups vegetable stock or broth

1 (28-ounce) can diced tomatoes, with liquid

¾ cup shell-shaped pasta

3 tablespoons tomato paste

2 bay leaves

1 teaspoon Italian seasoning

½ teaspoon salt

¼ teaspoon pepper

1 (14.5-ounce) can kidney beans, drained and rinsed

1 WITH the cooker's lid off, heat oil on HIGH or "brown," until sizzling.

2 PLACE the onion in the cooker, and sauté until lightly caramelized, about 5 minutes.

3 ADD carrots and celery, and sauté 1 minute.

4 ADD remaining ingredients, except for kidney beans. Securely lock the pressure cooker's lid and set for 6 minutes on HIGH.

5 PERFORM a quick release to release the cooker's pressure.

6 STIR in kidney beans. (You may wish to remove the bay leaves before serving.)

NUTRITION

Calories: 195

Fat: 5.5g

Total Carbs: 29.5g

Fiber: 6.5g

Protein: 9.5g

LIGHTER

White Chicken Chili

A Light, but Very Satisfying Chili Without Tomatoes

This recipe, chock-full of white navy beans and lean chicken meat, is just bursting with southwestern flavor—a fresh approach to a dish you already love.

SHOPPING LIST

1 cup small navy (white) beans (dry)

1 tablespoon vegetable oil

1 pound boneless, skinless chicken breasts, cubed

1 large yellow onion, chopped

1 green bell pepper, chopped

2 teaspoons chili powder

1 teaspoon ground cumin

1 teaspoon dry oregano

4 cups chicken stock or broth

Juice of 1 lime

1 tablespoon minced garlic

3 tablespoons chopped fresh cilantro

1 ½ cups frozen corn kernels

Salt and pepper

1 SOAK navy beans for 30 minutes as you prep the remaining ingredients. Drain and rinse the soaked beans.

2 WITH the cooker's lid off, heat oil on HIGH or "brown," until sizzling.

3 PLACE the chicken and onion in the cooker, and cook until chicken is lightly browned, 5–7 minutes.

4 ADD remaining ingredients, securely lock the pressure cooker's lid, and set for 20 minutes on HIGH.

5 LET the pressure release naturally 10 minutes before performing a quick release for any remaining pressure.

6 ADD salt and pepper to taste before serving.

NUTRITION

Calories: 340

Fat: 9g

Total Carbs: 34.5g

Fiber: 10.5g

Protein: 32g

LIGHTER

Tangy Lentil Salad

Bright, Light, and Filling

Lentils have to be one of the healthiest foods around—high in protein, fiber, and iron. In this delightful easy-to-make salad, celery, onion, and red bell pepper add a cooling crunch, while freshly squeezed lemon juice offers a bright and tangy bite.

SHOPPING LIST

1 cup dried lentils, rinsed

2 cups chicken stock or broth

½ teaspoon dried thyme

1 bay leaf

½ cup diced celery

¼ cup finely diced red onion

¼ cup finely diced red bell pepper

2 tablespoons extra virgin olive oil

Juice of 1 lemon

1 tablespoon minced garlic

2 tablespoons chopped fresh parsley

½ teaspoon dried oregano

¾ teaspoon salt

¼ teaspoon pepper

1 ADD lentils, chicken stock, thyme, and bay leaf to the cooker.

2 SECURELY lock the pressure cooker's lid and set for 8 minutes on HIGH.

3 PERFORM a quick release to release the cooker's pressure. Drain lentils and remove bay leaf.

4 COMBINE lentils with remaining ingredients. Serve warm or chilled.

NUTRITION

Calories: 165

Fat: 5g

Total Carbs: 21g

Fiber: 10g

Protein: 9g

LIGHTER

Barley Risotto

with Fresh Spinach

This creamy dish replaces rice with the nutty flavor of barley, and with a healthy dose of deliciously vitamin-rich spinach, you simply cannot go wrong.

SHOPPING LIST

1 tablespoon olive oil

1 tablespoon light margarine

1 yellow onion, diced

1 cup pearled barley

4 cups chicken stock or broth

Juice of 1 lemon

1 tablespoon minced garlic

4 cups baby spinach

¼ cup grated Parmesan cheese

Salt and pepper

NUTRITION

Calories: 195

Fat: 6g

Total Carbs: 30g

Fiber: 6g

Protein: 6g

1 WITH the cooker's lid off, heat oil and margarine on HIGH or "brown," until oil is sizzling and margarine is melted.

2 PLACE diced onion in the cooker, and sauté until translucent, 5 minutes.

3 STIR in barley, and sauté 1 additional minute.

4 ADD the chicken broth, lemon juice, and minced garlic. Securely lock the pressure cooker's lid and set for 22 minutes on HIGH.

5 LET the pressure release naturally 5 minutes before performing a quick release for any remaining pressure.

6 WITH the cooker's lid off, set to HIGH or "brown," and stir in spinach and Parmesan cheese, simmering until spinach cooks down. Season with salt and pepper to taste before serving.

LIGHTER

Whole-Wheat Pasta Primavera

with Chicken and Colorful Vegetables

This vibrant dish marries the fresh flavors of whole-wheat rotini, protein-packed chicken breast, peas, carrots, bell pepper, and Parmesan cheese for a complete and well-balanced meal.

SHOPPING LIST

1 tablespoon olive oil

2 boneless, skinless chicken breasts, cubed

1 red onion, diced

2 cups whole-wheat rotini pasta

2 cups chicken stock or broth

½ teaspoon Italian seasoning

¼ teaspoon garlic powder

2 cups frozen peas and carrots mix, thawed

¼ cup finely diced red bell pepper

¼ cup grated Parmesan cheese

1 tablespoon chopped fresh parsley

Salt and pepper

1 WITH the cooker's lid off, heat oil on HIGH or "brown," until sizzling.

2 PLACE chicken breasts and onion in the cooker, and sauté until chicken is browned and onion is translucent, about 5 minutes.

3 ADD pasta, chicken stock, Italian seasoning, and garlic powder. Securely lock the pressure cooker's lid and set for 6 minutes on HIGH.

4 PERFORM a quick release to release the cooker's pressure.

5 STIR in peas and carrots, red bell pepper, Parmesan cheese, and parsley. Add salt and pepper to taste before serving.

NUTRITION

Calories: 375

Fat: 8g

Total Carbs: 39g

Fiber: 6.5g

Protein: 36g

LIGHTER

Tender Stuffed Flank Steak

with Spinach and Parmesan Cheese

While this recipe requires a little more prepping than usual, just think of how many compliments you'll receive once the steaks have been rolled, beautifully browned, and sliced into perfect spirals.

SHOPPING LIST

1 (12-ounce) package frozen spinach, thawed

1 tablespoon minced garlic

¼ cup grated Parmesan cheese

1 flank steak (about 2 pounds)

Cooking twine

Salt and pepper

1 teaspoon paprika

½ teaspoon dried thyme

1 tablespoon olive oil

⅔ cup beef stock or broth

NUTRITION

Calories: 340

Fat: 15g

Total Carbs: 3g

Fiber: 1.5g

Protein: 45.5g

1 DRAIN thawed spinach well, squeezing out all water. Combine spinach, garlic, and Parmesan cheese to create the filling.

2 SLICE flank steak in half horizontally, opening like a book. Lay out 4 lengths of cooking twine and place flank steak on top. Season the inside generously with salt and pepper, and then add the filling mixture over top. Roll the flank steak up, and tie twine.

3 SEASON the outside of stuffed steak with salt, pepper, paprika, and thyme.

4 WITH the cooker's lid off, heat oil on HIGH or "brown," until sizzling. Place stuffed steak in the cooker, and sauté until browned.

5 ADD beef stock to the cooker, securely lock the lid, and set for 30 minutes on HIGH.

6 LET the cooker's pressure release naturally for 5 minutes before performing a quick release to release any remaining pressure. Let rest 5 minutes before serving.

LIGHTER

Rubbed Pork Tenderloin

with Peach Salsa

Served alongside a good amount of fresh peach salsa made from scratch (to add a cooling touch of sweetness), this spice-rubbed pork tenderloin adds a bit of flavor to your week without too much of a hassle.

SHOPPING LIST

2 teaspoons vegetable oil

1 (1 ½-pound) pork tenderloin

2 teaspoons chili powder

1 teaspoon paprika

¼ teaspoon garlic powder

¾ teaspoon salt

½ teaspoon pepper

1 cup chicken stock or broth

2 peaches, pitted and diced

⅓ cup diced red onion

Juice of 1 lime

1 tablespoon chopped fresh cilantro

2 teaspoons minced garlic

NUTRITION

Calories: 300

Fat: 9g

Total Carbs: 7.5g

Fiber: 1.5g

Protein: 45.5g

1 WITH the cooker's lid off, heat oil on HIGH or "brown," until sizzling.

2 IN a small bowl or ramekin, combine chili powder, paprika, garlic powder, salt, and pepper. Rub the mixture evenly onto all sides of the pork, and place in the cooker, cooking until lightly browned.

3 ADD the chicken stock to the cooker, and securely lock the pressure cooker's lid. Set for 20 minutes on HIGH.

4 LET the cooker's pressure release naturally for 10 minutes before quick releasing any remaining pressure.

5 COMBINE the peaches, onion, lime juice, cilantro, and garlic to create the salsa.

6 REMOVE roast, and let rest under aluminum foil 10 minutes before carving and serving topped with the salsa.

Chicken with Stewed Cherry Tomatoes

Clean Mediterranean Flavors Made Easy

With this dish, eating smart takes very little effort, tossing in the simple yet sophisticated flavors of cherry tomatoes and black olives. If you are a true olive lover like I am, then try taking it even further by substituting kalamata olives instead!

SHOPPING LIST

1 tablespoon olive oil

4 boneless, skinless chicken breasts

1 red onion, thinly sliced

2 pints cherry tomatoes

½ cup chicken stock or broth

1 ½ teaspoons Italian seasoning

¼ teaspoon garlic powder

⅛ teaspoon salt

⅛ teaspoon pepper

¼ cup chopped black olives

NUTRITION

Calories: 305

Fat: 9g

Total Carbs: 9.5g

Fiber: 2.5g

Protein: 50g

1 WITH the cooker's lid off, heat oil on HIGH or "brown," until sizzling.

2 PLACE chicken breasts in oil in the cooker, and cook until browned on both sides. Use tongs to remove chicken from the cooker and set aside.

3 PLACE onion in the cooker, and cook until translucent, 4–5 minutes.

4 RETURN chicken to the cooker, and cover with remaining ingredients, stirring to combine.

5 SECURELY lock the pressure cooker's lid and set for 8 minutes on HIGH.

6 PERFORM a quick release to release the cooker's pressure. Serve each chicken breast smothered with a heaping spoonful of the olives, tomatoes, and onions.

LIGHTER

Chipotle Chicken

Low in Calories, High in Flavor

Chipotle chiles are known for their smoky, spicy flavor. Here, they have a starring role, but not without a little fat-free sour cream to cut some of that heat.

SHOPPING LIST

1 tablespoon olive oil

4 boneless, skinless chicken breasts

Salt and pepper

½ cup chicken stock or broth

2 tablespoons diced chipotle chiles in adobo sauce

1 teaspoon light brown sugar

¼ teaspoon garlic powder

1 tablespoon chopped fresh cilantro

Juice of ½ lime

2 teaspoons cornstarch, mixed into 1 tablespoon water

⅔ cup fat-free sour cream

1 tomato, diced

1 WITH the cooker's lid off, heat oil on HIGH or "brown," until sizzling.

2 SEASON chicken breasts with a generous amount of salt and pepper, place in the cooker, and sauté until browned.

3 ADD chicken stock, chiles, brown sugar, garlic powder, cilantro, and lime juice. Securely lock the pressure cooker's lid and set for 8 minutes on HIGH.

4 PERFORM a quick release to release the cooker's pressure.

5 WITH the cooker's lid off, set to HIGH or "brown." Add cornstarch mixture, and simmer for 2 minutes, until sauce is thickened.

6 STIR in sour cream and diced tomato before serving.

NUTRITION

Calories: 350

Fat: 7.5g

Total Carbs: 10g

Fiber: 0g

Protein: 54g

LIGHTER

Turkey and Vegetable Meatloaf

Extra-Lean Ground Turkey Stuffed with Moist Vegetables

While ground turkey, especially the extra lean kind used in this recipe, has a tendency to dry out, stuffing it with water-filled vegetables and cooking in a pressure environment ensures that the results are tender and moist.

SHOPPING LIST

2 pounds extra lean ground turkey

¼ cup Italian bread crumbs

½ cup diced yellow onion

½ cup diced zucchini

¼ cup diced red bell pepper

1 tablespoon minced garlic

1 teaspoon dried thyme

⅛ teaspoon ground allspice

1 teaspoon salt

½ teaspoon pepper

1 (8-ounce) can tomato sauce

½ cup chicken stock or broth

1 tablespoon cider vinegar

1 tablespoon light brown sugar

½ teaspoon Italian seasoning

1 IN a large mixing bowl, combine ground turkey, bread crumbs, onion, zucchini, red bell pepper, garlic, thyme, allspice, salt, and pepper. Form the mixture into a round loaf, small enough to fit into your pressure cooker.

2 ADD tomato sauce and chicken stock to the cooker, and top with the rounded meatloaf. Securely lock the pressure cooker's lid and set for 15 minutes on HIGH.

3 LET the cooker's pressure release naturally for 10 minutes before quick releasing any remaining pressure. Serve topped with sauce from the cooker.

NUTRITION

Calories: 310

Fat: 4g

Total Carbs: 13.5g

Fiber: 2g

Protein: 55g

LIGHTER

Tender Pears

in a Warm Raspberry Sauce

These tender, "poached" pears are served warm in a sweet and tangy raspberry sauce. For an even greater treat, try serving topped with a scoop of low-fat frozen yogurt!

SHOPPING LIST

4 pears, peeled, cored, and cut in half

⅔ cup apple juice

1 pint fresh raspberries

⅛ teaspoon vanilla extract

½ cup light brown sugar

1 tablespoon cornstarch, mixed into 1 tablespoon water

NUTRITION

Calories: 230

Fat: 0.5g

Total Carbs: 60g

Fiber: 10g

Protein: 1.5g

1 PLACE all ingredients, except brown sugar, in the pressure cooker and securely lock the pressure cooker's lid. Set for 7 minutes on LOW.

2 PERFORM a quick release to release the cooker's pressure. Remove pears and set aside.

3 USE a potato masher or heavy spoon to mash the raspberries in the cooker until nearly puréed.

4 WITH lid off, set cooker to HIGH or "brown," and stir in brown sugar and cornstarch mixture. Let simmer 3 minutes, or until sauce has thickened.

5 RETURN pears to the sauce to coat before serving drizzled in additional sauce.

LIGHTER

Poached Peach Cups

with Ricotta and Honey

Even if you aren't looking for healthier alternatives, this dessert is exceptional, infused with the flavors of apples, brown sugar, and cinnamon, and then topped with honey and vanilla ricotta cheese.

SHOPPING LIST

4 peaches, cut in half and pitted

¼ cup apple juice

¼ cup water

3 tablespoons light brown sugar

⅛ teaspoon ground cinnamon

1 cup part-skim ricotta cheese

2 tablespoons honey

¼ teaspoon vanilla extract

NUTRITION

Calories: 190

Fat: 5g

Total Carbs: 29.5g

Fiber: 1.5g

Protein: 8g

1 ADD peaches, apple juice, water, brown sugar, and cinnamon to the cooker.

2 SECURELY lock the pressure cooker's lid and set for 4 minutes on LOW.

3 PERFORM a quick release to release the cooker's pressure.

4 REMOVE peaches from cooking liquid, and set aside.

5 COMBINE ricotta cheese, honey, and vanilla extract, and serve spooned into the center of each peach half.

LIGHTER

Real Steel-Cut Oatmeal

with Cinnamon and Brown Sugar

Steel-cut oats, heartier and chewier than rolled oats, are one of my favorite things to make in a pressure cooker. Traditionally taking as long as thirty minutes to make, this version cooks in only five minutes.

SHOPPING LIST

3 tablespoons light margarine

1 cup steel-cut oats

3 ½ cups water

½ teaspoon ground cinnamon

¼ teaspoon salt

¼ cup low-fat milk

¼ cup (or more to taste) light brown sugar

1 WITH the cooker's lid off, heat margarine on HIGH or "brown," until melted.

2 ADD the oats, water, cinnamon, and salt. Securely lock the pressure cooker's lid and set for 5 minutes on HIGH.

3 PERFORM a quick release to release the cooker's pressure.

4 STIR in milk and brown sugar and serve immediately.

NUTRITION

Calories: 215

Fat: 6.5g

Total Carbs: 37g

Fiber: 4g

Protein: 6.5g

LIGHTER

HOLIDAY COOKING

Cranberry Meatballs

A Super Simple Holiday Appetizer

When it comes to the holidays, there simply is no better time to pull out the pressure cooker. These sweet and slightly tangy meatballs will save some of that precious stove-top space you'll need for the rest of the meal.

SHOPPING LIST

1 tablespoon vegetable oil

1 yellow onion, diced

32 ounces frozen meatballs

½ cup beef stock or broth

1 (18-ounce bottle) barbecue sauce

1 (16-ounce) can jellied cranberry sauce

1 teaspoon lemon zest

HELPFUL TIP

When using an electric pressure cooker, you can set the cooker to warm and serve these meatballs right out of the pot with no worries of it cooling down.

1 WITH the cooker's lid off, heat oil on HIGH or "brown," until sizzling.

2 PLACE onion in the cooker, and cook until translucent, 4–5 minutes.

3 ADD remaining ingredients, securely lock the pressure cooker's lid, and set for 8 minutes on HIGH.

4 PERFORM a quick release to release the cooker's pressure. Serve meatballs with plenty of sauce.

HOLIDAY

Sweet Potato Casserole

A Traditional Favorite, Simplified

Cooked until smooth and rich and creamy and then sprinkled with a good amount of chopped pecans, this take on the holiday classic is everything you know and love, just without crowding up the oven.

SHOPPING LIST

8 cups thick-cubed sweet potatoes

3 tablespoons butter or margarine, melted

¾ cup water

¾ teaspoon vanilla extract

½ teaspoon ground cinnamon

⅛ teaspoon ground nutmeg

⅛ teaspoon salt

¾ cup light brown sugar

1 tablespoon cornstarch

⅓ cup heavy cream

½ cup chopped pecans

1 ADD sweet potatoes, butter, water, vanilla extract, cinnamon, nutmeg, salt, and brown sugar to the cooker.

2 SECURELY lock the pressure cooker's lid and set for 4 minutes on HIGH.

3 PERFORM a quick release to release the cooker's pressure.

4 WHISK together cornstarch and heavy cream, and gently stir into cooked sweet potatoes. Let simmer for 2 minutes.

5 SERVE topped with pecan pieces.

MAKE IT BETTER

Serve topped with a dollop of marshmallow fluff for a quick and easy alternative to marshmallow-topped casseroles.

HOLIDAY

Moist Stuffing from Scratch

Turkey's Favorite Sidekick

It always seems there isn't enough room to cook the traditional holiday staples. Since stuffing is a must, why not make it moist and quick in the pressure cooker? That'll clear a spot in your oven or on your stove for something else.

SHOPPING LIST

1 tablespoon vegetable oil

1 large yellow onion, diced

1 cup chopped celery

8 cups dry cubed bread crumbs

3 cups chicken stock or broth

2 large eggs, beaten

4 tablespoons butter, melted

¾ teaspoon poultry seasoning

1 ½ tablespoons chopped fresh sage

¾ teaspoon dried thyme

¾ teaspoon sugar

¾ teaspoon salt

¼ teaspoon pepper

1 WITH the cooker's lid off, heat oil and onion on HIGH or "brown," and sauté until onion is translucent.

2 ADD remaining ingredients to the cooker, and toss well to coat bread crumbs.

3 SECURELY lock the pressure cooker's lid and set for 13 minutes on LOW.

4 PERFORM a quick release to release the cooker's pressure. Serve immediately.

MAKE IT YOURS

This basic recipe can be expanded by adding a handful of dried cranberries or chopped pecans.

HOLIDAY

Stuffed Turkey Cutlets

with Green Beans, Cranberries, and Pecans

Using cutlets instead of the whole bird and rolling the usual side dishes right into these Stuffed Turkey Cutlets saves quite a bit of time and energy, yet still keeps holiday traditions intact.

SHOPPING LIST

8 turkey cutlets, about ¼ inch thick

Salt and pepper

3 cups fresh green beans, trimmed

1 tablespoon butter, melted

1 tablespoon minced garlic

1 tablespoon chopped fresh sage

¼ cup dried cranberries

¼ cup chopped pecans

1 cup chicken stock or broth

1 teaspoon paprika

½ teaspoon poultry seasoning

HELPFUL TIP

If your store does not carry turkey cutlets, try asking your butcher if they can thinly slice a turkey tenderloin.

1 SEASON both sides of turkey cutlets with a generous amount of salt and pepper.

2 COMBINE green beans, melted butter, garlic, sage, cranberries, and pecans to create the filling.

3 ADD an equal amount of the filling to the center of each turkey cutlet. Roll up cutlets, and secure with toothpicks.

4 FOR best results, place a small metal rack or trivet at the bottom of your pressure cooker.

5 POUR in chicken stock, place stuffed cutlets on rack, and sprinkle with paprika and poultry seasoning. Securely lock the pressure cooker's lid and set for 10 minutes on HIGH.

6 PERFORM a quick release to release the cooker's pressure. Let rest 5 minutes before serving.

HOLIDAY

Parsnip and Rutabaga Mash

with Cinnamon, Brown Sugar, and Nutmeg

Parsnips and rutabagas are two often overlooked root vegetables that can bring something new and unique to your table, especially for the holidays. Here, they are mashed into one very special side dish, absolutely singing with familiar fall spices.

SHOPPING LIST

1 pound parsnips, peeled and chopped 1 ½ inches thick

1 pound rutabagas, peeled and chopped 1 ½ inches thick

2 cups water

4 tablespoons butter

2 tablespoons half-and-half

2 tablespoons light brown sugar

¼ teaspoon ground cinnamon

1 small pinch ground nutmeg

½ teaspoon salt

1 PLACE the parsnips, rutabagas, and water in the pressure cooker, securely lock the cooker's lid, and set for 5 minutes on HIGH.

2 PERFORM a quick release to release the cooker's pressure.

3 DRAIN cooked vegetables and return to the pot. Using a heavy fork or potato masher, mash parsnips and rutabagas until mostly smooth, adding all remaining ingredients as you go. Serve immediately.

MAKE IT EASIER

This can also be made with carrots or sweet potatoes in place of the rutabaga, as rutabagas are not the easiest thing to chop.

HOLIDAY

Spiced Rice Pilaf

A Twist on Rice Pilaf Fit for the Holidays

More and more, people are looking for new dishes to introduce to their holiday spreads. As this version of rice pilaf offers classic holiday flavors, it will surely complement all the old traditions.

SHOPPING LIST

2 tablespoons butter or margarine

1 tablespoon vegetable oil

1 yellow onion, diced

2 ribs celery, diced

⅓ cup finely diced red bell pepper

2 cups long-grain white
rice (uncooked)

½ teaspoon ground allspice

⅛ teaspoon ground cinnamon

½ teaspoon salt

¼ teaspoon pepper

2 ¼ cups vegetable stock or broth

1 tablespoon light brown sugar

⅓ cup chopped pecans

1 WITH the cooker's lid off, heat the butter, oil, and onion on HIGH or "brown," until butter is melted and onion is translucent.

2 ADD the celery, red bell pepper, rice, allspice, cinnamon, salt, and pepper to the cooker, and sauté 1 minute.

3 POUR in vegetable stock, securely lock the pressure cooker's lid, and set for 4 minutes on HIGH.

4 PERFORM a quick release to release the cooker's pressure.

5 STIR in brown sugar and pecans before serving.

MAKE IT YOURS

Dried cranberries or raisins can be added in the last step to add even more classic holiday flavors.

HOLIDAY

Eggnog Rice Pudding

Spiced to Sweet Perfection

The holidays simply wouldn't be the holidays without eggnog around, and with this rice pudding, you can enjoy it in an entirely new way.

SHOPPING LIST

2 tablespoons butter or margarine

1 cup Arborio or Calrose rice

2 cups water

½ teaspoon vanilla extract

¼ teaspoon rum extract

⅛ teaspoon ground nutmeg

⅛ teaspoon ground cinnamon

1 ½ cups eggnog

⅓ cup light brown sugar

MAKE IT BETTER

I like to add a handful of raisins after cooking and top each serving with a pinch of cinnamon.

1 WITH the cooker's lid off, heat butter on HIGH or "brown," until melted.

2 POUR the rice in the cooker, and sauté 1 minute.

3 ADD the water, vanilla extract, rum extract, nutmeg, and cinnamon. Securely lock the pressure cooker's lid and set for 6 minutes on HIGH.

4 PERFORM a quick release to release the cooker's pressure.

5 STIR in eggnog and brown sugar before serving.

HOLIDAY

Figgy Bread Pudding

with Walnuts and Orange Zest

While most people don't quite know what Figgy Pudding is, this modernized version will give a pretty good idea as to what those carolers in that song are going on and on about.

SHOPPING LIST

Nonstick cooking spray

5–6 cups torn old or crusty bread

1 ½ cups chopped fresh figs

⅓ cup chopped walnuts

5 large eggs

½ cup heavy cream

1 ½ cups milk

½ cup sugar

3 tablespoons butter or margarine, melted

1 tablespoon all-purpose flour

2 teaspoons orange zest

1 teaspoon vanilla extract

⅛ teaspoon ground cinnamon

MAKE IT MEMORABLE

Chocolate goes great with the figs and orange zest in this recipe, so I like to drizzle with chocolate syrup before serving.

1 SPRAY 2 (5-inch) metal cake pans or 1 (2-quart) soufflé dish with nonstick cooking spray.

2 TOSS together torn bread, figs, and walnuts, and add to the pans or dish, filling to the very top.

3 WHISK together remaining ingredients, and pour over top of the dry ingredients in the pans or dish, pressing the bread down to saturate. Let sit 10 minutes.

4 PLACE a small metal rack or trivet at the bottom of your pressure cooker. Pour 2 cups of water into the bottom of the cooker to create a water bath.

5 COVER pans or dish with aluminum foil, and place on metal rack in cooker (stacking the 2 cake pans).

6 SECURELY lock the cooker's lid and set for 25 minutes on HIGH.

7 LET the pressure release naturally for 10 minutes before performing a quick release for any remaining pressure. Let rest 15 minutes before serving.

Croissant Bread Pudding

with Apples and Raisins

Buttery croissants, sweet dried apples, raisins, and cinnamon make this one-of-a-kind dessert a perfect choice to sweeten up the holidays.

SHOPPING LIST

Nonstick cooking spray

5–6 cups torn croissants

1 cup dried apples, chopped

½ cup raisins

5 large eggs

½ cup heavy cream

1 ½ cups milk

½ cup light brown sugar

2 tablespoons butter or margarine, melted

1 tablespoon all-purpose flour

1 teaspoon ground cinnamon

MAKE IT MEMORABLE

Serve drizzled with a quick sauce made from ¼ cup light brown sugar, 3 tablespoons melted butter, and a pinch of cinnamon.

1 SPRAY 2 (5-inch) metal cake pans or 1 (2-quart) soufflé dish with nonstick cooking spray.

2 TOSS together torn croissants, dried apples, and raisins, and add to the pans or dish, filling to the very top.

3 WHISK together remaining ingredients, and pour over top of the dry ingredients in the pans or dish, pressing the croissants down to saturate. Let sit 10 minutes.

4 PLACE a small metal rack or trivet at the bottom of your pressure cooker. Pour 2 cups of water into the bottom of the cooker to create a water bath.

5 COVER pans or dish with aluminum foil, and place on metal rack in cooker (stacking the 2 cake pans).

6 SECURELY lock the cooker's lid and set for 25 minutes on HIGH.

7 LET the pressure release naturally for 10 minutes before performing a quick release for any remaining pressure. Let rest 15 minutes before serving.

Apple Cranberry Chutney

with Chopped Pecans

Chutney is often served alongside turkey as a sweet and chunky, complementary sauce. Sticking with traditions is a must in this case, as the holidays simply aren't the same without apples and cranberries around.

SHOPPING LIST

1 (12-ounce) bag fresh cranberries

2 apples, peeled, cored, and chopped

1 cup sugar

⅔ cup apple juice

⅛ teaspoon ground cinnamon

1 tablespoon cornstarch, mixed into 2 tablespoons water

½ cup chopped pecans

MAKE IT BETTER

Adding 2 teaspoons orange zest and a handful of raisins before serving will liven up this chutney even further.

1 PLACE cranberries, apples, sugar, apple juice, and cinnamon in the cooker, and securely lock the pressure cooker's lid. Set for 5 minutes on HIGH.

2 PERFORM a quick release to release the cooker's pressure.

3 WITH the lid off, set cooker to HIGH or "brown," and stir in cornstarch mixture. Let simmer 3 minutes, or until sauce has thickened.

4 USE a potato masher or heavy spoon to mash ⅓ of the cranberries in the cooker.

5 STIR in pecans and serve warm.

HOLIDAY

DESSERTS

Most Moist Brownies

with Chocolate Chips and Pecan Bits

These moisture-rich brownies may not be square anymore, but they'll certainly satisfy any sweet tooth.

SHOPPING LIST

Nonstick cooking spray

1 stick butter, melted

1 cup sugar

1 large egg

1 teaspoon vanilla extract

½ cup all-purpose flour

⅓ cup unsweetened cocoa powder

½ cup chopped pecans

⅓ cup semisweet chocolate chips

HELPFUL TIP

As the pans you will be making this in are most likely round, your best option is to cut them into slices like a cake...I promise they will still taste like brownies though!

1 SPRAY 2 (5-inch) metal cake pans with non-stick cooking spray.

2 WHISK together melted butter, sugar, egg, and vanilla extract.

3 IN a separate bowl, combine flour and cocoa powder, and then whisk the liquid ingredients into the dry.

4 FOLD pecans and chocolate chips into the batter, and then transfer to the metal cake pans.

5 FOR best results, place a small metal rack at the bottom of your pressure cooker. Pour 2 cups of water into the bottom of the cooker to create a water bath.

6 STACK the 2 cake pans on top of each other, and place on metal rack in cooker. Cover top pan with a metal cover or aluminum foil to keep moisture out.

7 SECURELY lock the cooker's lid and set for 25 minutes on HIGH.

8 LET the pressure release naturally for 10 minutes before performing a quick release for any remaining pressure. Let rest for 10 minutes before serving warm.

DESSERT

Mango Shortcakes

A Sunny Fruit-Topped Treat Dolloped with Whipped Cream

Mangos offer a tropical approach to this familiar dessert, served warm over shortcakes or slices of pound cake.

SHOPPING LIST

3 mangos, peeled and cubed

½ cup mango nectar

¼ cup water

⅓ cup sugar

¼ teaspoon vanilla extract

1 ½ tablespoons cornstarch, mixed into 2 tablespoons water

Shortcakes or sliced pound cake

Whipped cream

HELPFUL TIP

Many stores now sell precut mango in the refrigerated produce case. Though it will cost more money than peeling your own, it is a very good option when the store's fresh mangos feel too soft.

1 PLACE mangos, mango nectar, water, sugar, and vanilla extract in the cooker.

2 SECURELY lock the pressure cooker's lid and set for 2 minutes on HIGH.

3 PERFORM a quick release to release the cooker's pressure.

4 WITH the cooker's lid off, set to HIGH or "brown." Stir in cornstarch mixture, and simmer for 2 minutes, just until thickened.

5 SPOON mangos and sauce over shortcakes or pound cake slices, and serve topped with whipped cream.

DESSERT

Blueberry Cinnamon Sundae Sauce

Serve Over Ice Cream, Pound Cake, Pancakes, or Waffles

With a few handfuls of blueberries, a dash or two of cinnamon, and a whole lot of sweetness, a little drizzle of this can brighten up any dessert or breakfast treat.

SHOPPING LIST

2 cups frozen blueberries

⅔ cup purple grape juice

½ cup water

¼ teaspoon ground cinnamon

½ cup light brown sugar

1 tablespoon cornstarch, mixed into 2 tablespoons water

MAKE IT MEMORABLE

This makes particularly good fresh blueberry shortcakes. Simply top shortcake or dessert biscuits with this sauce, whipped cream, and a handful of fresh blueberries to garnish.

1 PLACE blueberries, grape juice, water, and cinnamon in the cooker, and securely lock the pressure cooker's lid. Set for 7 minutes on LOW.

2 PERFORM a quick release to release the cooker's pressure.

3 USE a potato masher or heavy spoon to mash the blueberries in the cooker until nearly puréed.

4 WITH lid off, set cooker to HIGH or "brown," and stir in brown sugar and cornstarch mixture. Let simmer 3 minutes, or until sauce has thickened.

5 SERVE warm or chilled over ice cream, pound cake, pancakes, waffles, or other goodies.

DESSERT

Chocolate and Coconut Rice Pudding

Like a Favorite Candy Bar

One of my favorite desserts to make in a pressure cooker is rice pudding, and with the added flavors of rich chocolate syrup and tropical coconut shreds, it's by far and away a better alternative than just grabbing a candy bar.

SHOPPING LIST

2 tablespoons butter or margarine

1 cup Arborio or Calrose rice

2 cups water

½ teaspoon vanilla extract

1 (14-ounce) can coconut milk

1 cup shredded sweetened coconut

⅓ cup sugar

Chocolate syrup

MAKE IT YOURS

Any kind of chocolate can be used in place of the chocolate syrup in this recipe. I would suggest mini chocolate chips (which melt into the pudding) or hot fudge.

1 WITH the cooker's lid off, heat butter on HIGH or "brown," until melted.

2 POUR the rice in the cooker, and sauté 1 minute.

3 ADD the water and vanilla extract, securely lock the pressure cooker's lid, and set for 6 minutes on HIGH.

4 PERFORM a quick release to release the cooker's pressure.

5 WITH the pressure cooker's lid off, stir in coconut milk, shredded coconut, and sugar.

6 PLACE in serving bowls, drizzle each with chocolate syrup, and serve warm.

DESSERT

Banana Bottomed Flan

Spanish Custard with Fresh Bananas

This flan combines rich custard with all the flavors of Bananas Foster. This is also the perfect way to use an overly ripened banana, as those will have the most flavor.

SHOPPING LIST

3 tablespoons butter or margarine, melted

3 tablespoons light brown sugar

1 ½ large bananas, sliced

1 cup water

2 large eggs

7 ounces (½ can) sweetened condensed milk

6 ounces (½ can) evaporated milk

¼ teaspoon banana extract

¼ teaspoon vanilla extract

PLAY IT SAFE

After cooking, with the pressure cooker's lid off, let the flan cool for at least 15 minutes before attempting to remove. Always use pot holders!

1 WHISK together butter and brown sugar, and then pour into a 5- to 7-inch metal cake or pie pan that is small enough to fit into your pressure cooker. Coat the entire bottom of the pan with the mixture and top with a layer of the sliced bananas.

2 FOR best results, place a small metal rack at the bottom of your pressure cooker.

3 POUR 1 cup of water into the pressure cooker to create a water bath.

4 WHISK together all remaining ingredients to create the flan mixture. Pour the mixture over the bananas in the metal pan until about 1 ¾ inches high. (You may have enough flan mixture to create 2 batches.) Bananas should float to the top of the pan. If your pie pan has a metal cover, cover now.

5 PLACE pie pan over rack in pressure cooker, securely lock the cooker's lid, and set for 17 minutes on HIGH.

6 LET the pressure release naturally for 10 minutes before performing a quick release for any remaining pressure.

7 REFRIGERATE for a minimum of 3 hours before running a knife around the edges and inverting onto a plate to serve.

DESSERT

S'mores Bread Pudding

A Fireside Treat, All Grown Up

There's no need for logs and matches for this play on s'mores, and while there is still that ooey-gooey appeal, your fingers won't get all sticky.

SHOPPING LIST

Nonstick cooking spray

5–6 cups torn, hearty wheat bread

⅔ cup semisweet chocolate chips

5 large eggs

½ cup heavy cream

1 ½ cups milk

½ cup sugar

1 tablespoon butter or margarine, melted

1 tablespoon honey

1 tablespoon all-purpose flour

1 teaspoon vanilla extract

⅛ teaspoon ground cinnamon

Marshmallow fluff

MAKE IT BETTER

If you happen to own a kitchen torch, you can make this even more authentic.

1 SPRAY 2 (5-inch) metal cake pans or 1 (2-quart) soufflé dish with nonstick cooking spray.

2 TOSS together torn bread and chocolate chips, and add to the pans or dish, filling to the very top.

3 WHISK together remaining ingredients, except marshmallow fluff, and pour over top of the dry ingredients in the pans or dish, pressing the bread down to saturate. Let sit 10 minutes.

4 PLACE a small metal rack or trivet at the bottom of your pressure cooker. Pour 2 cups of water into the bottom of the cooker to create a water bath.

5 COVER pans or dish with aluminum foil, and place on metal rack in cooker (stacking the 2 cake pans).

6 SECURELY lock the cooker's lid and set for 25 minutes on HIGH.

7 LET the pressure release naturally for 10 minutes before performing a quick release for any remaining pressure. Let rest 10 minutes, and then serve topped with a dollop of marshmallow fluff.

DESSERT

Cherries Jubilee

Serve Over Ice Cream, Pound Cake, or Both

Although typically made with liqueur and flambéed, this version has been simplified, still maintaining that tart yet sweet, cherry-packed flavor. Don't forget the vanilla ice cream!

SHOPPING LIST

16 ounces frozen cherries

½ cup orange juice

¼ cup water

¼ cup sugar

½ teaspoon orange zest

¼ teaspoon almond extract

¼ cup light brown sugar

1 tablespoon cornstarch, mixed into 2 tablespoons water

MAKE IT BETTER

Be sure to use natural almond extract in this recipe, not the "artificial" kind. Almonds and cherries share a similar flavor compound and natural almond extract will enhance the flavor of the cherries.

1 PLACE cherries, orange juice, water, sugar, orange zest, and almond extract in the cooker, and securely lock the pressure cooker's lid. Set for 7 minutes on LOW.

2 PERFORM a quick release to release the cooker's pressure.

3 USE a potato masher or heavy spoon to mash half of the cherries in the cooker to create a chunky sauce.

4 WITH the lid off, set cooker to HIGH or "brown," and stir in brown sugar and cornstarch mixture. Let simmer 3 minutes, or until sauce has thickened.

5 SERVE warm or chilled over ice cream, pound cake, or both.

Perfected Cheesecake

Rich and Creamy Dessert Perfection

Cheesecakes are one of the world's oldest desserts, and it's no wonder they are still just as craved for. Pressure cookers are a natural substitution for baking, as the pot conveniently serves as a built-in water bath.

SHOPPING LIST

Nonstick cooking spray

CRUST:

¾ cup graham cracker crumbs

2 tablespoons butter, melted

FILLING:

1 pound cream cheese, at room temperature

⅓ cup ricotta cheese

¾ cup sugar

3 large eggs

1 tablespoon lemon juice

¾ teaspoon vanilla extract

MAKE IT MEMORABLE

Be sure to serve this topped with whipped cream and freshly sliced strawberries for a perfect presentation.

1 SPRAY 2 (5-inch) metal cake pans (springform preferred) with nonstick cooking spray. Combine graham cracker crumbs and melted butter to create the Crust, and press an equal amount into the bottom of each cake pan.

2 USING an electric beater, mixer, or food processer, beat all Filling ingredients together on medium speed, just until well combined. Pour an equal amount of the Filling over top the Crust in each cake pan.

3 FOR best results, place a small metal rack at the bottom of your pressure cooker. Pour 2 cups of water into the bottom of the cooker to create a water bath.

4 STACK the 2 cake pans on top of each other and place on metal rack in cooker. Cover top pan with a metal cover or aluminum foil to keep moisture out.

5 SECURELY lock the cooker's lid and set for 25 minutes on HIGH.

6 LET the pressure release naturally for 10 minutes before performing a quick release for any remaining pressure. Let cool uncovered 1 hour before refrigerating at least 6 hours before serving.

DESSERT

Peanut Butter Cheesecake

Smooth...Creamy...Peanut Buttery!

This delightfully nutty version of cheesecake compares in texture to that of the baked kind, which also usually requires a water bath. The only real difference here is the simple fact that you can dig in sooner.

SHOPPING LIST

Nonstick cooking spray

CRUST:

½ cup graham cracker crumbs

¼ cup chopped peanuts

2 tablespoons butter, melted

FILLING:

1 pound cream cheese, at room temperature

⅔ cup natural peanut butter

¾ cup sugar

3 large eggs

¾ teaspoon vanilla extract

MAKE IT BETTER

To make a truly decadent cheesecake (as pictured at left), spread a layer of peanut butter over the cooled cake, and sprinkle peanut butter and chocolate morsels over top before serving.

1 SPRAY 2 (5-inch) metal cake pans (springform preferred) with nonstick cooking spray. Combine graham cracker crumbs, peanuts, and melted butter to create the Crust, and press an equal amount into the bottom of each cake pan.

2 USING an electric beater, mixer, or food processer, beat Filling ingredients together on medium speed, just until well combined. Pour an equal amount of the Filling over top the Crust in each cake pan.

3 FOR best results, place a small metal rack at the bottom of your pressure cooker. Pour 2 cups of water into the bottom of the cooker to create a water bath.

4 STACK the 2 cake pans on top of each other, and place on metal rack in cooker. Cover top pan with a metal cover or aluminum foil to keep moisture out.

5 SECURELY lock the cooker's lid and set for 25 minutes on HIGH.

6 LET the pressure release naturally for 10 minutes before performing a quick release for any remaining pressure. Let cool uncovered 1 hour before refrigerating at least 6 hours before serving.

DESSERT

Prep Time	Cook Time	Temperature	Serves
20 min	25 min	High	8

Tangerine Cheesecake

with a Pecan Cookie Crust

Chopped pecans and bright, tangy tangerines make this already addictive dessert even harder to return to the refrigerator.

SHOPPING LIST

Nonstick cooking spray

CRUST:

½ cup crushed sandy pecan cookies

¼ cup chopped pecans

2 tablespoons butter, melted

FILLING:

1 pound cream cheese, at room temperature

⅓ cup ricotta cheese

¾ cup sugar

3 large eggs

1 tablespoon lemon juice

2 teaspoons tangerine zest

1 teaspoon vanilla extract

MAKE IT BETTER

Top with additional chopped pecans, and drizzle with melted white chocolate to make this cheesecake even more extraordinary.

1 SPRAY 2 (5-inch) metal cake pans (springform preferred) with nonstick cooking spray. Combine crushed cookies, pecans, and melted butter to create the Crust, and press an equal amount into the bottom of each cake pan.

2 USING an electric beater, mixer, or food processer, beat all Filling ingredients together on medium speed, just until well combined. Pour an equal amount of the Filling over top the Crust in each cake pan.

3 FOR best results, place a small metal rack at the bottom of your pressure cooker. Pour 2 cups of water into the bottom of the cooker to create a water bath.

4 STACK the 2 cake pans on top of each other, and place on metal rack in cooker. Cover top pan with a metal cover or aluminum foil to keep moisture out.

5 SECURELY lock the cooker's lid and set for 25 minutes on HIGH.

6 LET the pressure release naturally for 10 minutes before performing a quick release for any remaining pressure. Let cool uncovered 1 hour before refrigerating at least 6 hours before serving.

BEEF

TYPE	SIZE	LIQUID	TIME	TEMP	RELEASE	FROZEN
Brisket	2–3 lbs	Covered	70 min	High	Natural	n/a
Brisket	4–5 lbs	Covered	85 min	High	Natural	n/a
Chuck Roast	3–4 lbs	2 cups	70 min	High	Natural	n/a
Corned Beef	2–3 lbs	Covered	70 min	High	Natural	n/a
Corned Beef	4–5 lbs	Covered	85 min	High	Natural	n/a
Flank Steak	2–3 lbs	1 cup	25 min	High	Natural	+8 min
Ground Beef	1–2 lbs	⅔ cup	5 min	High	Quick	n/a
Oxtails	Any	Covered	45 min	High	Natural	n/a
Rib Roast	3–4 lbs	2 cups	60 min	High	Natural	n/a
Round Roast	3–4 lbs	2 cups	70 min	High	Natural	n/a
Shanks	Any	1 ½ cups	45 min	High	Natural	n/a
Short Ribs	Any	1 ½ cups	30 min	High	Natural	+10 min
Shoulder Roast	3–4 lbs	2 cups	70 min	High	Natural	n/a
Steak, Thin	1-inch thick	⅔ cup	20 min	High	Quick	+5 min
Stew Meat	1-inch cubes	1 cup	20 min	High	Natural	+8 min

CHICKEN

TYPE	SIZE	LIQUID	TIME	TEMP	RELEASE	FROZEN
Breasts, with Bone	Any	½ cup	12 min	High	Quick	+8 min
Breasts, Boneless	Any	½ cup	8 min	High	Quick	+7 min
Cornish Hen	2 hens	1 cup	14 min	High	Natural	+10 min
Ground Chicken	Any	⅔ cup	5 min	High	Quick	n/a
Leg Quarters	2 lbs	1 cup	14 min	High	Natural	+10 min

TYPE	SIZE	LIQUID	TIME	TEMP	RELEASE	FROZEN
Thighs	2 lbs	⅔ cup	8 min	High	Quick	+8 min
Whole Chicken	3–4 lbs	2 cups	30 min	High	Natural	+15 min
Wings	2–3 lbs	⅔ cup	8 min	High	Quick	n/a

PORK

TYPE	SIZE	LIQUID	TIME	TEMP	RELEASE	FROZEN
Baby Back Ribs	1 rack	1 cup	20 min	High	Natural	n/a
Chops	½-inch	½ cup	8 min	High	Quick	+7 min
Chops	1-inch	½ cup	15 min	High	Natural	+10 min
Ham Hocks	Any	Covered	50	High	Natural	n/a
Ham Steaks	2–4 steaks	½ cup	6 min	High	Quick	+5 min
Ham, Whole	3–5 lbs	3 cups	40 min	High	Natural	+25 min
Loin Roast	2–4 lbs	2 cups	45 min	High	Natural	n/a
Roast	3–5 lbs	2 cups	80 min	High	Natural	n/a
Roast, 2-inch sliced	3–5 lbs	2 cups	55 min	High	Natural	n/a
Sausages	Any	Covered	10 min	High	Quick	+7 min
Spareribs	2–4 lbs	1 cup	20 min	High	Natural	n/a

OTHER MEATS

TYPE	SIZE	LIQUID	TIME	TEMP	RELEASE	FROZEN
Lamb Chops	½-inch	½ cup	6 min	High	Quick	+5 min
Lamb Chops	1-inch	½ cup	12 min	High	Quick	+7 min
Lamb Leg	3–4 lbs	2 cups	45 min	High	Natural	+20 min
Lamb Shanks	Any	1 ½ cups	30 min	High	Natural	+10 min
Turkey Breast	3–5 lbs	2 cups	40 min	High	Natural	+15 min

OTHER MEATS CONTINUED

TYPE	SIZE	LIQUID	TIME	TEMP	RELEASE	FROZEN
Turkey Legs	2–4 legs	1 ½ cups	20 min	High	Natural	+10 min
Veal Roast	3–4 lbs	2 cups	60 min	High	Natural	+20 min
Veal Shanks	Any	1 ½ cups	25 min	High	Natural	n/a
Veal Steaks	½-inch	½ cup	6 min	High	Quick	+7 min
Venison Roast	3–4 lbs	2 cups	50 min	High	Natural	+20 min
Venison Stew Meat	1-inch cubes	1 ½ cups	30 min	High	Natural	+10 min

SEAFOOD

TYPE	SIZE	LIQUID	TIME	TEMP	RELEASE	FROZEN
Clams	Any	1 cup	5 mins	High	Quick	n/a
Cod	Any	½ cup	5 mins	High	Quick	+4 min
Crab Legs	Small	1 cup	3 mins	High	Quick	n/a
Lobster Tail	½ pound	1 cup	5 mins	High	Quick	+4 min
Mussels	Any	1 cup	3 mins	High	Quick	n/a
Salmon	Any	½ cup	6 mins	High	Quick	+5 min
Scallops, Bay	Any	½ cup	1 min	High	Quick	+2 min
Scallops, Sea	Any	½ cup	2 min	High	Quick	+1 min
Shrimp	Medium	½ cup	2 min	High	Quick	+2 min
Shrimp	Jumbo	½ cup	3 min	High	Quick	+4 min
Tilapia	Any	½ cup	5 min	High	Quick	+4 min

VEGETABLES

TYPE	SIZE	LIQUID	TIME	TEMP	RELEASE	FROZEN
Acorn Squash	Halved	1 cup	5 min	High	Quick	n/a
Artichokes	Whole	1 cup	9 min	High	Quick	n/a

VEGETABLES CONTINUED

TYPE	SIZE	LIQUID	TIME	TEMP	RELEASE	FROZEN
Asparagus	Thick	½ cup	2 min	Low	Quick	n/a
Beets	Sliced	¾ cup	5 min	High	Quick	n/a
Brussels Sprouts	Any	½ cup	2 min	High	Quick	n/a
Butternut Squash	Cubed	1 cup	3 min	High	Quick	n/a
Cabbage	Quartered	Covered	3 min	High	Quick	n/a
Carrots	Any	½ cup	4 min	High	Quick	n/a
Corn on the Cob	Any	1 cup	3 min	High	Quick	n/a
Eggplant	Chopped	½ cup	4 min	Low	Quick	n/a
Green Beans	Any	½ cup	2 min	Low	Quick	n/a
Potatoes, New	Whole	1 cup	3 min	High	Quick	n/a
Potatoes, Russet	Thick Cut	1 cup	3 min	High	Quick	n/a
Potatoes, Sweet	Thick Cut	1 cup	3 min	High	Quick	n/a
Rutabaga	Cubed	1 cup	4 min	High	Quick	n/a
Squash, Yellow	Thick Cut	½ cup	2 min	Low	Quick	n/a
Turnip	Cubed	½ cup	4 min	High	Quick	n/a
Zucchini	Thick Cut	½ cup	2 min	Low	Quick	n/a

BEANS AND LEGUMES

TYPE	SIZE	LIQUID	TIME	TEMP	RELEASE	FROZEN
Black Beans	Any	Covered	20 min	High	Natural	n/a
Black-Eyed Peas	Any	Covered	8 min	High	Natural	n/a
Cannellini	Any	Covered	35 min	High	Natural	n/a
Garbanzo	Any	Covered	35 min	High	Natural	n/a
Great Northern	Any	Covered	25 min	High	Natural	n/a
Kidney	Any	Covered	22 min	High	Natural	n/a
Lentils	Any	Covered	8 min	High	Quick	n/a

BEANS AND LEGUMES CONTINUED

TYPE	SIZE	LIQUID	TIME	TEMP	RELEASE	FROZEN
Lima	Any	Covered	12 min	High	Natural	n/a
Navy	Any	Covered	20 min	High	Natural	n/a
Peanuts, Raw	Any	Covered	75 min	High	Natural	n/a
Pinto	Any	Covered	22 min	High	Natural	n/a
Scarlet Runner	Any	Covered	16 min	High	Natural	n/a
Split Peas	Any	Covered	6 min	High	Quick	n/a

PASTA AND GRAINS

TYPE	SIZE	LIQUID	TIME	TEMP	RELEASE	FROZEN
Brown Rice, Short	Per Cup	2x	14 min	High	Quick	n/a
Brown Rice, Medium	Per Cup	2x	14 min	High	Quick	n/a
Brown Rice, Long	Per Cup	2x	10 min	High	Quick	n/a
Couscous	Per Cup	1 ½x	2 min	High	Quick	n/a
Orzo	Per Cup	3 ½x	4 min	High	Quick	n/a
Shaped Macaroni	Per Cup	2 ½x	6 min	High	Quick	n/a
Steel-Cut Oats	Per Cup	3 ½x	5 min	High	Quick	n/a
Tortellini, Dried	Per Cup	3x	5 min	High	Quick	n/a
White Rice, Short	Per Cup	2 ½x	6 min	High	Quick	n/a
White Rice, Medium	Per Cup	2x	5 min	High	Quick	n/a
White Rice, Long	Per Cup	1 ¾x	4 min	High	Quick	n/a

(handwritten notes)

* (cup that came ō cooker)
1 cup brown wild rice to 1½ cup H2O on brown rice setting

white rice too mooshy ō cooker menu use this

* 2 cups dried split peas = 1 lb

About the Author

Well-known TV personality **Bob Warden** has proven taste and sizzling passion for great food as a television cooking celebrity, kitchenware developer, and cookbook author. He is a hugely successful TV cooking show host, product developer, and QVC manufacturers' representative, with four decades of experience. Bob has helped develop more than 500 kitchen products for QVC, as well as for other top brand kitchen manufacturers. Bob's previous cookbooks include *Quick and Easy Pressure Cooking*, *Best of the Best Cook's Essentials Cookbook* (with Gwen McKee), and *Bob Warden's Slow Food Fast*. Warden's newest venture, Great Chefs International, includes the launch of a TV series, companion cookbook, and the premiere of Great Flavors, a new collection of low-sodium, high-taste concentrated stock bases.

About the Photography

The food photographs in this book were taken by **Christian and Elise Stella**, under the guidance of Bob Warden. All food in the photographs was purchased at an ordinary grocery store and prepared exactly to the recipe's directions. No artificial food styling techniques were used to "enhance" the food's appearance. Only water was sometimes spritzed on the food to keep it looking fresh during the thirty-minute photo shoots. No food prepared for photographs went to waste. All photographs were shot on a Canon 5dmkii with a Zeiss 35mm f/2 lens.

RECIPE INDEX

RECIPE INDEX CONTINUED